GW00702069

CROCHET

Jean Kinmond was Needlecraft and Fashion Adviser to Coats the internationally known threadmakers for thirty years. She previously taught at Harris Academy, Dundee.

Jean Kinmond has written many books including *Sewing – Teach Yourself*, and *Embroidery – Teach Yourself* published by Brockhampton Press and *Counted Thread Embroidery, Embroidery for the Home, The Anchor Book of European Embroidery, The Anchor Book of Lace Crafts, Crochet Patterns, Fashion Crochet* and *The Coats Book of Lace Crafts* published by Batsford.

TEACH YOURSELF BOOKS

CROCHET

Jean Kinmond

TEACH YOURSELF BOOKS
Hodder and Stoughton

First Edition 1979

Copyright © 1979
J. and P. Coats Ltd

Line drawings and photographs supplied by courtesy of J. and P. Coats Ltd. and Patons and Baldwins Ltd.

Published in the U.S.A. by David McKay & Co. Inc., 750 Third Avenue, New York, N.Y. 10017, U.S.A.

ISBN 0 340 24709 6

Printed and bound in Great Britain for Hodder and Stoughton paperbacks, a division of Hodder and Stoughton Ltd., Mill Road, Dunton Green, Sevenoaks, Kent, (Editorial Office; 47 Bedford Square, London, WC1B 3DP) by Richard Clay (The Chaucer Press) Ltd., Bungay, Suffolk

Contents

Introduction

Crochet is an old craft, though there is no accurate information about its history. The word crochet is the French word for hook and, as a hook is used in making crochet lace, this is strong evidence for associations with France.

Crochet was extensively produced in the convents of Europe during the sixteenth century and it was without doubt the nuns who carried the craft to Ireland, where it developed into an elaborate and distinctive form with patterns of rosettes, leaves and lace fillings.

Crochet became very popular in England during the reign of Victoria, as can be seen in the many pictures of the overpowering drawing rooms of the time, with heavy crochet antimacassars, mantelpiece covers with a fringing of heavy bobbles and many other crochet pieces.

The Victorian ladies have left us a heritage of delicate crochet laces worked in very fine cotton. These may be found in museums or are the treasured heirlooms of their descendants. How surprised and perhaps envious these ladies would be were they to see the wide range of yarns, both natural and synthetic, which are available today for the art of crochet. In Victorian times little was done in the field of fashion crochet. Today, with the use of bulkier yarns, combined with the expert styling of fashion designers, it is now possible to create a wardrobe of elegant yet practical garments for every member of the family. The interest in crochet is increasing and it is now one of the most popular crafts. The diagrams and instructions given in this book will enable the beginner to master all the basic crochet stitches and to work the selection of designs which follow.

Explanatory notes on the different types of crochet are given at the beginning of each section.

1

Crochet Stitches

It is suggested you learn to crochet with a wool or synthetic yarn equal in thickness to Double Knitting and then work an article in one of the thicker yarns. At the beginning, keep your stitches fairly loose and this will help you to see each stitch formation more clearly. Gradually, with practice, you will achieve the correct tension. Once you are proficient, it is certain you will be tempted to prove your skill by working a piece of crochet lace.

Coats Chain Mercer-Crochet Cotton is the perfect yarn for crochet lace. It is fine and is produced in a range of sizes and colours, see p. 25. It has a mercerised finish and is firm, and so retains the clarity and traditional delicacy of the patterns. One important point, cotton is less elastic than wool, and in order to produce a satisfactory texture, fine crochet hooks as quoted must be used. Remember to keep the working thread fairly tight and the tension even and regular.

Note: When changing from wool or synthetic yarn to cotton, it is advisable to work a practice piece first to establish the change over.

Stitch Diagrams

The shading on each stitch diagram denotes the foundation chain stitches and the number of turning chain stitches used at the end of the row.

Position of Thread and Hook (Fig. 1). Grasp yarn near one end of ball between thumb and forefinger of left hand. With right hand form yarn into loop. Hold loop in place between thumb and forefinger of left hand.

With right hand take hold of broad bar of hook as you would a pencil. Insert hook through loop and under yarn. With right hand, catch long end of yarn (Fig. 2).

Fig. 1   Fig. 2

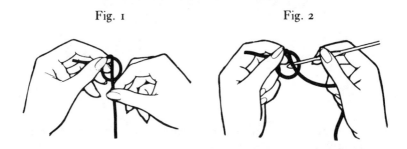

Draw loop through but do not remove hook from yarn. Pull short end in opposite direction to bring loop close round the end of the hook (Fig. 3).

Loop yarn round little finger, across palm and behind forefinger of left hand. Grasp hook and loop between thumb and forefinger of left hand. Pull yarn gently so that it lies round the fingers firmly (Fig. 4).

Fig. 3   Fig. 4

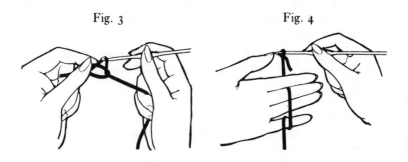

Catch knot of loop between thumb and forefinger. Hold broad bar of hook with right hand as described in Fig. 2 (Fig. 5).

Pass hook under yarn and catch yarn with hook. This is called 'yarn over'. Draw yarn through loop on hook. This makes one chain (Fig. 6).

Fig. 5   Fig. 6

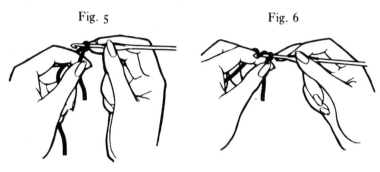

Chain – *ch*

This is the foundation of crochet work. With yarn in position and the loop on the hook as shown in Fig. 5, pass the hook under the yarn held in left hand and catch yarn with hook (Fig. 7), draw yarn through loop on hook, repeat this movement until chain is desired length (Fig. 8).

Fig. 7   Fig. 8

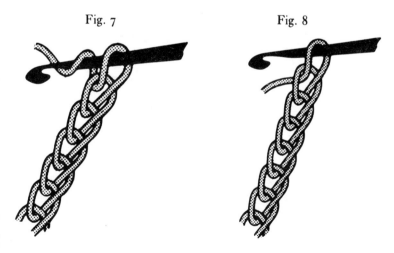

Slip Stitch – ss

Insert hook into stitch to left of hook, catch yarn with hook and draw through stitch and loop on hook (Fig. 9).

Fig. 9

Double Crochet – dc

Insert hook into 2nd stitch to left of hook, catch yarn with hook (Fig. 10) draw through stitch (2 loops on hook) (Fig. 11), yarn over hook and draw through 2 loops on hook (1 loop remains on hook) (Fig. 12). Continue working into each stitch to left of hook.

Fig. 10

Fig. 11

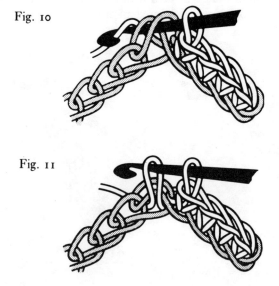

Fig. 12

Half Treble – hlf tr

Pass hook under the yarn held in left hand (Fig. 13), insert hook into 3rd stitch to left of hook, yarn over hook and draw through stitch (3 loops on hook), yarn over hook (Fig. 14), draw yarn through all loops on hook (1 loop remains on hook) (Fig. 15). Continue working into each stitch to left of hook.

Fig. 13

Fig. 14

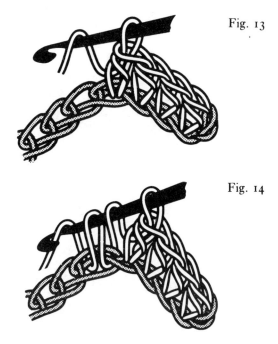

Fig. 15

Treble – tr

Pass hook under the yarn of left hand (Fig. 16), insert hook into 4th stitch to left of hook, yarn over hook and draw through stitch (3 loops on hook), yarn over hook (Fig. 17), and draw through 2 loops on hook, yarn over hook (Fig. 18), and draw through remaining 2 loops (1 loop remains on hook) (Fig. 19). Continue working into each stitch to left of hook.

Fig. 16

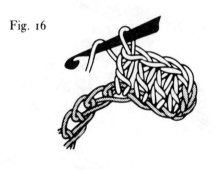

Fig. 17

Fig. 18

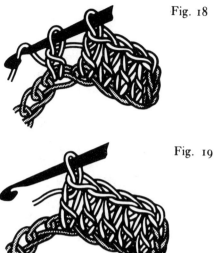

Fig. 19

Double Treble – dbl tr

Pass hook under the yarn of left hand twice, insert hook into 5th stitch to left of hook, yarn over hook and draw through stitch (4 loops on hook) (Fig. 20), yarn over hook and draw through 2 loops on hook, yarn over hook and draw through other 2 loops on hook, yarn over hook and draw through remaining 2 loops (1 loop remains on hook). Continue working into each stitch to left of hook.

Fig. 20

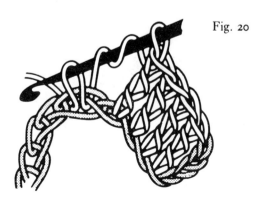

Triple Treble – trip tr

Pass hook under the yarn of left hand 3 times, insert hook into 6th stitch to left of hook, yarn over hook and draw through stitch (5 loops on hook) (Fig. 21), yarn over hook and draw through 2 loops on hook, (yarn over hook and draw through other 2 loops on hook) 3 times (1 loop remains on hook). Continue working into each stitch to left of hook.

Fig. 21

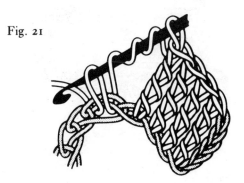

Quadruple Treble – quad tr

Pass hook under the yarn of left hand 4 times, insert hook into 7th stitch to left of hook and complete in same manner as trip tr until only 1 loop remains (Fig. 22).

Fig. 22

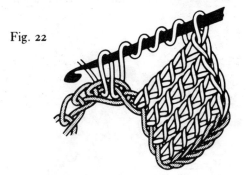

Space(s) – sp(s)

Filet Crochet: The following four stitches are used mostly in

Filet Crochet and are referred to as spaces and blocks, lacets and bars. Spaces may be made with 2 ch, miss 2 stitches, 1 tr into next stitch (Fig. 23).

Fig. 23

Block(s) – blk(s) and Space – (sp)
1 tr into 4th stitch to left of hook, 1 tr into each of next 2 stitches, 2 ch, miss 2 stitches, 1 tr into next stitch, 1 tr into each of next 3 stitches (Fig. 24).

Fig. 24

Bar and Lacet
(a) A bar consists of 5 ch, miss 5 stitches or a lacet, 1 tr into next stitch.
(b) A lacet consists of 3 ch, miss 2 stitches, 1 dc into next stitch, 3 ch, miss 2 stitches, 1 tr into next stitch (Fig. 25).

Fig. 25

Picot – *p*

Make a ch of 3, 4 or 5 stitches according to length of picot desired, then join ch to form a ring by working 1 dc into first ch (Fig. 26).

Fig. 26

Cluster(s) – *cl(s)*

Leaving the last loop of each on hook, work 2, 3 or more tr or dbl tr into same stitch, yarn over hook and draw through all loops on hook (Fig. 27).

Joining Circle with a Slip Stitch

Make a ch of 6 stitches. Join with a ss into first ch to form a ring (Fig. 28).

Fig. 27

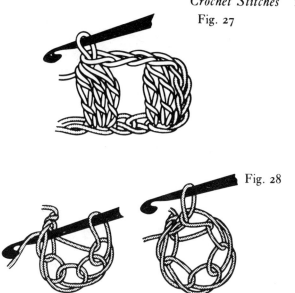

Fig. 28

Popcorn Stitch

1 ch, 5 tr into next stitch, remove loop from hook, insert hook into 1 ch before group of treble then into dropped loop and draw it through (Fig. 29).

Fig. 29

Solomon's Knot

Draw a loop on hook out 6 mm ($\frac{1}{4}$ in), yarn over hook and draw through loop on hook. Insert hook between loop and single thread of this ch and make a dc. Work another knot in same manner (1 Solomon's Knot made), miss 4 stitches, 1 dc into next stitch. Rep from beginning to end of row. Make 1$\frac{1}{2}$ Solomon's Knots to turn, 1 dc over double loop at right of first centre knot of preceding row, 1 dc over double loop at left of same knot, 1 Solomon's Knot. Rep to end of row (Fig. 30).

Fig. 30

Puff Stitch

Commence with a length of ch having a multiple of 2 ch plus 1. *1st Row:* 1 tr into 4th ch from hook * yarn over hook, insert hook into next ch and draw yarn up 1 cm ($\frac{3}{8}$ in) (yarn over hook, insert hook into same ch and draw yarn up as before) 3 times, yarn over and draw through all loops on hook (a puff st made), 1 ch, miss 1 ch; rep from * to last 3 ch, a puff st into next ch, 1 tr into each of next 2 ch, 3 ch, turn (Fig. 31).

Fig. 31

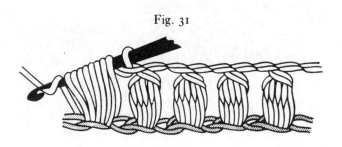

Crossed Treble

Commence with a length of ch, having a multiple of 4 ch plus 2.
1st Row: 1 dbl tr into 5th ch from hook, * yarn over hook twice, insert
hook into next ch and draw yarn through, yarn over hook and draw
through 2 loops, yarn over hook, miss 1 ch, insert hook into next ch
and draw yarn through, (yarn over hook and draw through 2 loops)
4 times, 1 ch, 1 tr into centre point of cross (cross completed), 1 ch,
miss 1 ch; rep from * to last 2 ch, 1 dbl tr into each of next 2 ch, 4
ch, turn (Fig. 32).

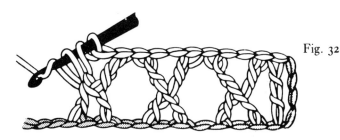

Fig. 32

Turning Work

In general, crochet patterns are worked row by row from right to
left and the work is turned at the end of each row. A certain number
of chain stitches are added at the end or beginning of each row to
bring the work into position for the next row: the number of
turning chain depends upon the stitch with which you intend to
begin the next row. However, certain articles such as doilies and
circular mats are worked from the centre, commencing with a ring
of chain stitches and so there is no need to turn the work unless
specifically directed in the instructions.

2

General Information

Abbreviations

beg – beginning

blk(s) – block(s)

ch – chain

cm – centimetres

D – dark

dc – double crochet

dec – decreasing

dbl tr – double treble

gr(s) – group(s)

hlf tr – half treble

in – inches

inc – increasing

L – light

m – metres

m – medium

patt – pattern

quad tr – quadruple treble

quin tr – quintuple treble

rep – repeat

sp(s) – space(s)

ss – slip stitch

st(s) – stitch(es)

tr – treble

trip tr – triple treble

Tension

Tension means the number of rows and stitches measured over a given area of crochet fabric. Correct tension is essential if you are to obtain the quoted size of the article and the degree of firmness or lacyness of the texture. This is particularly important in the field of garment size. To obtain satisfactory results it is advisable to use the quoted yarn and hook size. If your crochet is loose use a size finer hook, if tight use a size larger hook.

* Asterisk

Repeat instructions following the asterisk as many more times as specified in addition to the original.

Repeat instructions in parenthesis as many times as specified. For example, '(4 ch, 1 dc into next sp) 3 times', means to make all that is in parenthesis 3 times in all.

It is advisable to purchase at one time the number of balls sufficient for your requirements.

Laundering Mercer-Crochet

Mercer-Crochet colours are fast dyed and are highly resistant to even the most severe washing treatments but these colours may be adversely affected when washed in certain commercial washing preparations which contain high levels of fluorescent brightening (whitening) agents. To maintain the true tones of Mercer-Crochet colours it is recommended that pure soap flakes type washing agents be used as these generally contain only low concentrations of fluorescent brightening (whitening) agents.

Crochet items should not be washed when work is still in progress. The assembled article should be washed on completion.

Make a warm lather of pure soap flakes and wash in the usual way, either by hand or washing machine. If desired, the article may be spin-dried until it is damp, or left until it is half dry. Place a piece of paper, either plain white or squared, on top of a clean, flat board. Following the correct measurements, draw the shape of the finished article on to the paper, using ruler and set square for squares and rectangles and a pair of compasses for circles. Using rustless pins, pin the crochet out to the pencilled shape, taking care not to strain the crochet. Pin out the general shape first, then finish by pinning each picot, loop or space into position. Special points to note carefully when pinning out are:

(a) When pinning loops, make sure the pin is in the centre of each loop to form balanced lines.
(b) When pinning scallops, make all the scallops the same size and regularly curved.
(c) Pull out all picots.
(d) Where there are flowers, pull out each petal in position.
(e) When pinning filet crochet, make sure that the spaces and blocks are square and that all edges are even and straight.

If the crochet requires to be slightly stiffened, use a solution of starch – 1 dessertspoonful to $\frac{1}{2}$ litre (1 pint) hot water, and dab lightly over the article. Raise the crochet up off the paper, to prevent it sticking as it dries. When dry, remove the pins and press the article lightly with a hot iron.

Coats Mercer-Crochet Cotton 50 g balls

This thread is now available in a limited shade range in ticket No. 20. The shades are as follows: White, 402 (Lt. Rose Pink), 442 (Mid Buttercup), 469 (Geranium), 503 (Coral Pink), 508 (Lt. Marine Blue), 573 (Laurel Green), 582 (Straw Yellow), 608 (Tussah), 609 (Ecru), 610 (Dk. Ecru), 612 (Lt. Amethyst), 621 (Lt. French Blue), 625 (Lt. Beige), 884 (Shaded Pink), 889 (Shaded Lavender), 897 (Shaded Yellow).

White, 609 (Ecru) and 610 (Dk. Ecru) are also available in ticket No. 3, 10 and 40. For larger articles this may be a more economical purchase.

Sewing thread recommendation

When making up or finishing articles by hand or by machine, use the multi-purpose sewing thread Coats Drima (polyester). This thread is fine, yet very strong and is obtainable in a wide range of shades. Fine/Medium Fabrics, e.g. Linen or Cotton, use Machine

Needle No. 14 (British) 90 (Continental); No. of stitches to the cm (in) 4–5 (10–12); Milward Hand Needle No. 7 or 8.

Twisted cord

This is a simple cord to make, but care should be taken to see that it is firmly and evenly twisted as it tends to relax slightly in use.

Method. Measure off a number of threads, three times the length required for the finished cord, and fold them in half.

If someone is helping you to make the cord, a pencil can now be fixed to each end. Alternatively, if you are working alone, one end can be attached to a hook or pinned to some suitable place. Pull the threads and, keeping them quite taut, turn the pencil(s) round in the same direction as the twist of the thread. Continue until the cord is so tight that it begins to curl.

Still keeping the cord tight, place another pencil in the centre and double the cord over it till both ends meet. Next twist the cord in the opposite direction, until it begins to curl.

'Set' the cord by exerting a steady pull at both ends. This will cause it to stretch slightly and so retain its twist permanently.

Making a fringe

Cut 30·5 cm (12 in) lengths of yarn and taking eight strands together each time, knot into the end of each row to form a fringe. Press fringe and trim (Figs. 33a, b and c).

Fig. 33a

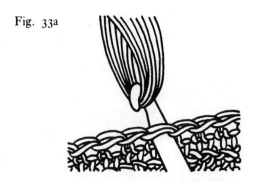

Fig. 33b

Fig. 33c

Increasing and decreasing at corners

This is a method of keeping work flat when the finished number of stitches does not interfere with the pattern.

To increase (inc)
Work two or more stitches into the foundation stitch.

To decrease (dec)
One method is merely to omit working into the foundation stitch, but this can result in a space being created in the work.

The most successful method is by making a joint stitch over two foundation stitches. A joint stitch is worked by leaving the last loop of next two stitches on hook (three loops on hook), yarn over hook and draw through all loops on hook.

Crochet Hooks

These are the correct numbers of steel hooks to use with Coats Mercer-Crochet:

	Milward Steel
Mercer-Crochet	Crochet hook
No. 3	1·75 (no. 2)
No. 10	1·50 (no. 2½)
No. 20 No. 30	1·25 (no. 3)
No. 40 No. 50	1·00 (no. 4)
No. 60	0·75 (no. 5)

British/American equivalents

The following table shows the nearest equivalent sizes of American crochet hooks. Before commencing an article work a tension sample and adjust hook size accordingly. (See paragraph 'Tension'):

British	*American*
0·60 (no. 6)	14 13
0·75 (no. 5)	12 11
1·00 (no. 4)	10 9
1·25 (no. 3)	8
1·50 (no. 2½)	7 6 5
1·75 (no. 2)	4 3 2
2·00 (no. 1)	1

British/American abbreviation equivalents

	British			*American*	
ch	(chain)		ch	(chain)	
dc	(double crochet)		sc	(single crochet)	
hlf tr	(half treble)		half dc	(half double crochet)	
tr	(treble)		dc	(double crochet)	
dbl tr	(double treble)		tr	(treble)	
trip tr	(triple treble)		dbl tr	(double treble)	
quad tr	(quadruple treble)		trip tr	(triple treble)	
ss	(slip stitch)		sl st	(slip stitch)	

3

Top

Popcorn stitch make the decorative bobbles on this attractive top.

Materials

13/14/15/16 (25 gram) balls of Patons Trident 4 ply.
For perfect results, use the recommended yarn.
Milward Disc (aluminium) crochet hooks 3·00 (no. 11) and 2·50 (no. 12).
The model illustrated is worked in shade 6718 (Snow-white).

Measurements

To fit bust 81/86/91/97 cm (32/34/36/38 in).
Length from top of shoulders, approximately 47/47/49/49 cm (18½/18½/19½/19½ in).
Sleeve seam 30/30/32/32 cm (12/12/12½/12½ in).

Tension

14 sts and 6 rows – 5 cm (2 in) measured over pattern using 3·00 (no. 11) hook.

Abbreviations   See p. 23.

Back and Front alike

With No. 2·50 hook, make 114/122/130/138 ch.
1st Row (wrong side):   1 dc in 2nd ch from hook, 1 dc in each remaining ch. 113/121/129/137 sts.

Change to No. 3·00 hook and work as follows.

2nd Row:　4 ch, miss first 2 sts, 1 tr in next st, * 1 ch, miss next st, 1 tr in next st; rep from * to end.

3rd Row:　4 ch, miss first 2 sts, 1 tr in next st, * 1 ch, miss next st, 1 tr in next st; rep from * ending 1 ch, miss next st, 1 tr in 3rd of 4 ch.

4th Row:　4 ch, miss first 2 sts, 1 tr in next st, (1 ch, miss next st, 1 tr in next st) 2/1/3/2 times, * 1 ch, miss next st, 5 tr in next st, remove loop from hook, insert hook in first tr of tr group and draw dropped loop through (a popcorn made) (1 ch, miss next st, 1 tr in next st) 5 times; rep from * ending last rep (1 ch, miss next st, 1 tr in next st) 3/2/4/3 times, 1 ch, miss next st, 1 tr in 3rd of 4 ch.

5th Row:　As 3rd.

6th Row:　4 ch, miss first 2 sts, (1 tr in next st, 1 ch, miss next st) 0/5/1/0 times, popcorn in next st, * (1 ch, miss next st, 1 tr in next st) 5 times, 1 ch, miss next st, popcorn in next st; rep from * ending (1 ch, miss next st, 1 tr in next st) 0/5/1/0 times, 1 ch, miss next st, 1 tr in 3rd of 4 ch.

3rd to 6th row forms patt.

Continue in patt until work measures 28 cm (11 in). Place a marker at each end of last row.

Now continue in patt until work measures approximately 43/43/45·5/45·5 cm (17/17/18/18 in), ending with a 3rd or 5th row of patt.

Work as follows:

If ending with 3rd patt row.

Next Row:　** 4 ch, miss 2 sts, (1 tr in next st, 1 ch, miss next st) 1/0/0/1 time, * popcorn in next st, 1 ch, miss next st, 1 tr in next st, 1 ch, miss next st; rep from * ending (popcorn in next st, 1 ch, miss next st) 0/1/1/0 time, 1 tr in 3rd of 4 ch. **

Next Row:　As 3rd row of patt.

Next Row:　*** 4 ch, miss 2 sts, (popcorn in next st, 1 ch, miss next st) 1/0/0/1 time, * 1 tr in next st, 1 ch, miss next st, popcorn in next st, 1 ch, miss next st; rep from * ending (1 tr in next st, 1 ch, miss next st) 0/1/1/0 time, 1 tr in 3rd of 4 ch. ***

Change to No. 2·50 hook and work 3 rows dc. Fasten off.

If ending with 5th patt row.

Next Row:　Work as for ending with 3rd patt row from *** to ***.

Next Row:　As 3rd row of patt.

Next Row: Work as for ending with 3rd patt row from ** to **.
Change to No. 2·50 hook and work 3 rows dc. Fasten off.

Sleeves

With No. 2·50 hook, make 106/106/118/118 ch.
1st Row (wrong side: 1 dc in 2nd ch from hook, 1 dc in
each remaining ch. 105/105/117/117 sts.
2nd and 3rd Rows: 1 ch, 1 dc in first st, 1 dc in each remaining st.
Change to No. 3·00 hook and work as follows:
4th Row: 4 ch, miss first 2 sts * popcorn in next st, 1 ch, miss next
st, 1 tr in next st, 1 ch, miss next st; rep from * ending popcorn in
next st, 1 ch, miss next st, 1 tr in last st.
5th Row: 4 ch, miss first 2 sts, 1 tr in next st, * 1 ch, miss next st, 1
tr in next st; rep from * ending 1 ch, miss next st, 1 tr in 3rd of 4th.
6th Row: 4 ch, miss first 2 sts, * 1 tr in next st, 1 ch, miss next st,
popcorn in next st, 1 ch, miss next st; rep from * ending 1 tr in next
st, 1 ch, miss next st, 1 tr in 3rd of 4 ch.
7th Row: As 5th.
8th Row: 4 ch, miss first 2 sts, 1 tr in next st, (1 ch, miss next st,
1 tr in next st) 3 times, * 1 ch, miss next st, popcorn in next st, (1 ch,
miss next st, 1 tr in next st) 5 times; rep from * ending last rep (1 ch,
miss next st, 1 tr in next st) 4 times, 1 ch, miss next st, 1 tr in 3rd of
4 ch.
9th Row: As 5th.
10th Row: 4 ch, miss first 2 sts, 1 tr in next st, * 1 ch, miss next st,
popcorn in next st, (1 ch, miss next st, 1 tr in next st) 5 times; rep
from * ending 1 ch, miss next st, popcorn in next st, 1 ch, miss next
st, 1 tr in next st, 1 ch, miss next st, 1 tr in 3rd of 4 ch.
7th to 10th row forms patt.

Continue in patt until sleeve seam measures 30·5/30·5/32/32 cm
(12/12/12$\frac{1}{2}$/12$\frac{1}{2}$ in). Fasten off.

To make up

Press parts very lightly on wrong side following instructions on the
ball band, taking care not to spoil the patt.

Join top edges of Back and Front, leaving 24/25·5/25·5/27 cm

($9\frac{1}{2}$/10/10/$10\frac{1}{2}$ in) open at centre for neck. Sew top edge of sleeves to side edges between markers, then join side and sleeve seams. Press seams.

Using 5 strands of yarn, make a twisted cord 137/142/147/152 cm (54/56/58/60 in) long or required length. Knot each end and fray ends to form tassels (See p. 26).

Thread cord through first row of holes at hem and tie at centre front.

Detail of Popcorn Stitch

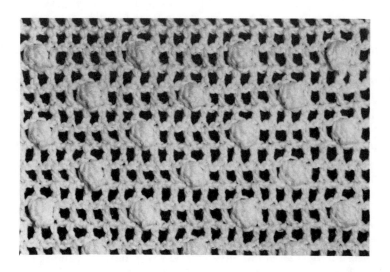

4

Girl's Pinafore

There are two sizes given in the instructions for this attractive pinafore, and although they are written for three colours, the design would look equally attractive using only the one colour.

Materials

3/5 (20 gram) balls of Patons Pennant Crêpe (knits as 4 ply) in Dark.

3/3 (20 gram) balls in Light and Medium.

For perfect results, use the recommended yarn.

Milward Disc (aluminium) crochet hook 3·50 (no. 9).

The model illustrated is worked in shades 725 (Snow-white), 2079 (Sunflower) and 687 (Saxon Blue).

Measurements

To fit 56/61 cm (22/24 in) chest.

Length from top of shoulder 40·5/47 cm (16/18 in).

Tension

5 groups of trebles – 7·5 cm (3 in).

6½ rows   – 5 cm (2 in).

Abbreviations   See p. 23.

Note: Carry yarns not in use loosely up side of work.

Back and Front Alike

With L, make 82/88 ch.

Foundation Row: In L, 1 tr in 4th ch from hook, * miss 2 ch, 3 tr in next ch; rep from * to last 3 ch, miss 2 ch, 2 tr in last ch. 25/27 grs with ½ gr at each end (starting ch counts as 1st tr on every row).

Work in patt as follows:

1st Row: In D, 3 ch, 3 tr in sp between ½ gr and 1st gr, 3 tr in each following sp between 2 gr ending 3 tr in sp between last gr and ½ gr, 1 tr in top of 3 ch. 26/28 grs with 1 tr at each end.

2nd Row: In M, 3 ch, 1 tr in sp between tr and 1st gr, 3 tr in each following sp, 2 tr in sp between last gr and 3 ch.

3rd Row: In L, as 1st.

4th Row: In D, as 2nd.

5th Row: In M, as 1st.

6th Row: In L, as 2nd.

These 6 rows form patt.

Work rows 1–3 again.

Shape as follows:

1st Shaping Row: 3 ch, 1 tr in 1st sp, 5/6 grs, 2 tr in next sp, 13 grs, 2 tr in next sp, patt to end.

2nd Shaping Row: 3 ch, 5/6 grs, 2 tr in each of next 2 sp, 12 grs, 2 tr in each of next 2 sps, patt to end.

3rd Shaping Row: 3 ch, 1 tr in 1st sp, 5/6 grs, 1 tr in next sp, 13 grs, 1 tr in next sp, patt to end.

4th Shaping Row: 3 ch, 5/6 grs, 1 tr in each of next 2 sps, 12 grs, 1 tr in each of next 2 sps, patt to end.

5th Shaping Row: In patt, but missing each sp between the 2 single tr, 23/25 grs with ½ gr at each end.

Work 2/4 rows straight.

Next Row: 3 ch, 5/6 grs, 2 tr in next sp, 12 grs, 2 tr in next sp, patt to end.

Next Row: 3 ch, 1 tr in 1st sp, 4/5 grs, 2 tr in each of next 2 sps, 11 grs, 2 tr in each of next 2 sps, patt to end.

Next Row: 3 ch, 5/6 grs, 1 tr in next sp, 12 grs, 1 tr in next sp, patt to end.

Next Row: 3 ch, 1 tr in 1st sp, 4/5 grs, 1 tr in each of next 2 sps, 11 grs, 1 tr in each of next 2 sps, patt to end.

Next Row: As 5th shaping row. 22/24 grs.

Work 2/4 rows straight.

Next Row: 3 ch, 1 tr in 1st sp, 4/5 grs, 2 tr in next sp, 11 grs, 2 tr in next sp, patt to end.

Next Row: 3 ch, 4/5 grs, 2 tr in each of next 2 sps, 10 grs, 2 tr in each of next 2 sps, patt to end.

Next Row: 3 ch, 1 tr in 1st sp, 4/5 grs, 1 tr in next sp, 11 grs, 1 tr in next sp, patt to end.

Next Row: 3 ch, 4/5 grs, 1 tr in each of next 2 sps, 10 grs, 1 tr in each of next 2 sps, patt to end.

Next Row: As 5th shaping row. 19/21 grs with $\frac{1}{2}$ gr at each end.

Work 2/4 rows straight.

Next Row: 3 ch, 4/5 grs, 2 tr in next sp, 10 grs, 2 tr in next sp, patt to end.

Next Row: 3 ch, 1 tr in 1st sp, 3/4 grs, 2 tr in each of next 2 sps, 9 grs, 2 tr in each of next 2 sps, patt to end.

Next Row: 3 ch, 4/5 grs, 1 tr in next sp, 10 grs, 1 tr in next sp, patt to end.

Next Row: 3 ch, 1 tr in 1st sp, 3/4 grs, 1 tr in each of next 2 sps, 9 grs, 1 tr in each of next 2 sps, patt to end.

Next Row: As 5th shaping row. 18/20 grs. Break all yarns.

Shape armholes as follows:

Next Row: Rejoin appropriate colour to sp between 3rd and 4th gr, 3 ch, 1 tr in this sp, 11/13 grs, 2 tr in next sp, turn.

Work 7/9 rows straight.

Shape neck and work straps as follows:

Next Row: 3 ch, 1 tr in 1st sp, 2 grs, 2 tr in next sp, turn.

Work straight until work measures 13/14 cm (5/5$\frac{1}{2}$ in) from start of armhole shaping. Fasten off.

Leaving 6/8 grs at centre unworked, rejoin appropriate colour to next sp, 3 ch, 1 tr in this sp, patt to end. Finish to correspond with 1st strap.

To make up

Using a cool iron and dry cloth, press parts on wrong side. Join side and shoulder seams.

Using D, work 1 row dc all round neck and armholes.

Lower Edge

1st Round: With right side facing, using M, work 1 round dc along lower edge by working 3 dc in each ch sp.

2nd Round: Using D, * 1 dc in each of next 3 dc, 5 ch, then work 1 dc into 1st of these 5 ch; rep from * to end of round. Fasten off.

Detail of Girl's Pinafore

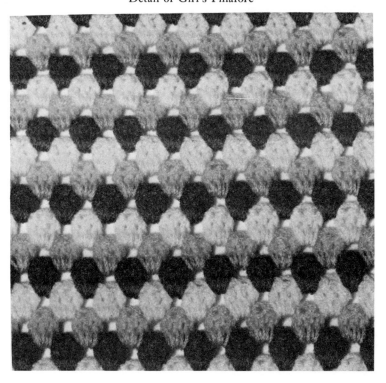

5

Scarf

This warm and cosy-looking scarf is a variation of the ever popular 'granny square'. The motif would make an equally attractive stole, blanket or pram cover.

This design is also ideally suitable for working in Coats Chain Mercer-Crochet Cotton No. 20, the size of each motif being 4 cm ($1\frac{1}{2}$ in) square, and would make attractive household articles, such as tray cloths, runners, tablecloths, etc.

Materials
4 (25 gram) balls of Patons Trident 4 ply in Dark.
5 (25 gram) balls each in Light and Medium.
For perfect results, use the recommended yarn.
Milward Disc (aluminium) crochet hook 3·00 (no. 11).
The model illustrated is worked in shades 462 (Dusky Brown), 104 (Lipstick Red) and 6728 (Amber).
Measurements
Width – 26 cm (10 in).
Length – 153 cm (60 in) excluding fringes.
Tension
Size of motif – 6·5 cm ($2\frac{1}{2}$ in) approximately.
Abbreviations See p. 23.

Motif A

With L make 4 ch and join into a ring with ss.

1st Row: In L, 3 ch, 2 tr, 1 ch, (3 tr, 1 ch) 3 times into ring, join with ss to top of ch.

2nd Row: In L, ss into 1st tr of previous row, 3 ch, 6 tr in same st, 1 ch, (7 tr, 1 ch in centre of next group of 3 tr) 3 times, join with ss to top of ch. Fasten off.

3rd Row: Join M to centre of 1st group of 7 tr, 3 ch 2 tr in this st, 1 ch, (3 dbl tr in ch sp of 1st row, working round ch sp of 2nd row as well, 1 ch, 3 tr, 2 ch, 3 tr all in centre of next group of 7 tr, 1 ch) 3 times, 3 dbl tr in ch sp of 1st row as before, 1 ch, 3 tr, 2 ch into first st of row, join with ss to top of ch. Fasten off.

4th Row: Join D to 1st 2 ch sp at corner, 3 ch 2 tr in this ch sp, 1 ch, * (3 tr,1 ch in next 1 ch sp) twice, 3 tr 2 ch 3 tr all in next 2 ch sp at corner, 1 ch; rep from * twice more, (3 tr, 1 ch in next 1 ch sp) twice, 3 tr 2 ch in 1st ch sp of row, join with ss to top of 4 ch. Fasten off.

Motif B

Work as Motif A but reading M for L and L for M.

Make 96 motifs – 48 each A and B.

To make up

Press motifs lightly on wrong side following instructions on the ball band. Alternating motifs A and B, join 4 together to form a strip.

Make 23 more strips the same.

Now join strips together alternating motifs. Press seams.

Fringes

Cut remaining L and M yarn into 30·5 cm (12 in) lengths and taking 8 strands together each time, knot into end of each row to form a thick fringe (See Fig. 33), alternating 1 tassel in L and 1 in M.

Detail of Scarf

6

Jacket

This easy to wear, edge to edge jacket in a simple pattern has no problems with fitting in the sleeves as they are worked in one with the main sections.

Materials

8/8/10/10 (25 gram) balls of Patons Trident Double Knitting in Dark.

8/8/8/8 (25 gram) balls each in Light and Medium.

For perfect results, use the recommended yarn.

Milward Disc (aluminium) crochet hooks 3·50 (no. 9) and 4·50 (no. 7). The model illustrated is worked in shades 6757 (Black), 50 (Cream) and 6755 (Sabre).

Measurements

To fit bust size 81/86/91/97 cm (32/34/36/38 in).

Length from top of shoulder 51/52/52/53 cm (20/20½/20½/21 in) approximately.

Sleeve seam 24 cm (9½ in) approximately.

Tension

4 groups of trebles and 7 rows – 7·5 cm (3 in).

Abbreviations   See p. 23.

Note: Join in and break off colours as required.

Back and Sleeves

With No. 4·50 hook and L, make 36 ch. Fasten off and leave for sleeve.

With No. 4·50 hook and D, make 70/76/79/85 ch.

1st Row (wrong side):   1 tr in 4th ch from hook, * miss 2 ch, 3 tr in next ch; rep from * ending last rep 2 tr in last ch. 21/23/24/26 groups of 3 tr.

** *2nd Row:*   In M, 3 ch, 3 tr in sp before first 3 tr, * 3 tr in sp before next 3 tr; rep from * ending 3 tr in sp after last 3 tr, 1 tr in top of 3 ch.

3rd Row: In L, 3 ch, 1 tr in first st, 3 tr in sp after first 3 tr, * 3 tr in sp after next 3 tr; rep from * ending 3 tr in sp before last 3 tr, 2 tr in top of 3 ch.

4th Row: In D, as 2nd.
5th Row: In M, as 3rd.
6th Row: In L, as 2nd.
7th Row: In D, as 3rd.

Note: 2nd to 7th row forms patt.

Work 2nd to 7th rows 3 times more, then 2nd row once, thus ending with wrong side facing for next row. **

Work Sleeves as follows:

Next Row: In L, make 39 ch, 1 tr in 4th ch from hook, (miss 2 ch, 3 tr in next ch) 11 times, 3 tr in next tr, patt to sp before last 3 tr, 3 tr in this sp, 3 tr in top of 3 ch, now work across 36 ch left at start of Back thus: (miss 2 ch, 3 tr in next ch) 11 times, miss 2 ch, 2 tr in last ch. 45/47/48/50 groups of 3 tr.

Continue in patt until Sleeve measures approximately 20/21·5/21·5/23 cm (8/8$\frac{1}{2}$/8$\frac{1}{2}$/9 in). Fasten off.

Left Front and Sleeve

With No. 4·50 hook and L, make 36 ch. Fasten off and leave.

*** With No. 4·50 hook and D, make 37/40/40/43 ch.

1st Row (wrong side):   1 tr in 4th ch from hook, * miss 2 ch, 3 tr in next ch; rep from * ending last rep 2 tr in last ch. 10/11/11/12 groups of 3 tr. ***.

Work as for Back from ** to **.

Work Sleeve as follows:

Next Row: In L, patt to sp before last 3 tr, 3 tr in this sp, 3 tr in top of 3 ch, now work across 36 ch left at start of Left Front thus: (miss 2 ch, 3 tr in next ch) 11 times, miss 2 ch, 2 tr in last ch. 22/23/23/24 groups of 3 tr.

Continue in patt until Sleeve measures approximately 13 cm (5 in) ending with right side facing for next row.

Shape neck as follows:

Next Row: 3 ch, 3 tr in sp before first 3 tr, (3 tr in sp before next 3 tr) 18/19/19/20 times, 1 tr in 2nd of next 3 tr, turn.

Continue in patt on these 19/20/20/21 groups of 3 tr until Front matches Back at sleeve edge. Fasten off.

Right Front and Sleeve

Work as for Left Front and Sleeve from *** to ***, then work as for Back from ** to **.

Work Sleeve as follows:

Next Row: In L, make 39 ch, 1 tr in 4th ch from hook, (miss 2 ch, 3 tr in next ch) 11 times, 3 tr in next tr, patt to end. 22/23/23/24 groups of 3 tr.

Continue in patt until Sleeve measures approximately 13 cm (5 in) ending with right side facing for next row. Break yarn.

Shape neck as follows:

Next Row: Leave first 2 tr and next 3 groups of 3 tr unworked, rejoin appropriate colour in 2nd of next 3 tr and make 3 ch, 3 tr in sp before next 3 tr, patt to end. 19/20/20/21 groups of 3 tr.

Continue in patt on these 19/20/20/21 groups of 3 tr until Front matches Back at sleeve edge. Fasten off.

To make up

Press parts lightly on wrong side following instructions on the ball band. Join upper seam of sleeves and shoulder seams, then join side seams and lower seam of sleeves.

Main Border

With right side facing, No. 3·50 hook and D, start at left side seam and work 1 round dc along lower edge, up right front, all round neck, down left front and along remainder of lower edge, inc and dec at corners as required (See p. 27).

Work another 2 rounds the same. Fasten off.

Sleeve Borders

With right side facing, No. 3·50 hook and D, work 3 rounds dc all round each sleeve. Fasten off.

Lightly press borders and seams.

Detail of Jacket

7

All-over Pattern Shawl

A pretty wrap for cool summer evenings or to enhance your outfit for a dance or theatre evening.

Materials
13 (25 gram) balls of Patons Trident 4 ply.
For perfect results, use the recommended yarn.
Milward Disc (aluminium) crochet hook 3·50 (no. 9).
The model illustrated is worked in shade 6743 (Larkspur).
Measurement
Depth at centre 68·5 cm (27 in) approximately.
Tension
1 repeat of pattern – 5 cm (2 in) in width.
Abbreviations   See p. 23.

Make 6 ch.
1st Row: Into first of these ch, work 5 tr then 1 dbl tr, turn.
2nd Row: Right side facing, 8 ch, then leaving the last loop of each on hook, work 3 trip tr in first st, yarn over and draw through all loops on hook (a 3 trip tr cluster made), (4 ch, miss 2 sts, a 3 trip tr cluster in next st) twice, (a leaf cluster made), 1 dbl tr in same place as last cluster.
3rd Row: 5 ch, 6 tr in first st, 3 ch, miss 1 cluster and 4 ch, 1 tr in

next cluster (1 tr made in centre of leaf cluster), 3 ch, 6 tr and 1 dbl tr in top of 8 ch.

4th Row: 8 ch, make a leaf cluster as before, miss 3 ch, 1 trip tr in next tr, miss 3 ch, make a leaf cluster as before over next 7 sts, 1 quad tr in same place as last cluster.

5th Row: 5 ch, 6 tr in first st, 3 ch, 1 tr in centre of leaf cluster, 3 ch, 7 tr in trip tr, 3 ch, 1 tr in centre of leaf cluster, 3 ch, 6 tr and 1 dbl tr in top of 8 ch.

6th Row: 8 ch, make a leaf cluster as before, * miss 3 ch, 1 trip tr in next tr, miss 3 ch, a leaf cluster as before over next 7 sts; rep from * 1 quad tr in same place as last cluster.

7th Row: 5 ch, 6 tr in first st, 3 ch, 1 tr in centre of leaf cluster, * 3 ch, 7 tr in trip tr, 3 ch, 1 tr in centre of leaf cluster; rep from * 3 ch, 6 tr and 1 dbl tr in top of 8 ch.

Rep 6th and 7th rows until work measures approximately 68·5 cm (27 in) at centre, ending with 6th row. Fasten off.

To make up

Press lightly following instructions on the ball band.

Fringe

Cut remaining yarn into 30·5 cm (12 in) lengths and taking 6 strands together each time, knot into end of each row to form fringe. Press fringe and trim (See Fig. 33 p. 26–7).

Detail of All-over Pattern Shawl

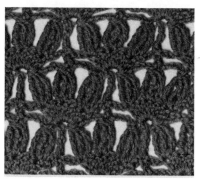

8

Blouse

This pretty blouse with diamond pattern would be suitable for both day or evening wear.

Materials

22/23 (20 gram) balls of Patons Fairytale Baby 3 ply.
For perfect results, use the recommended yarn.
Milward Disc (aluminium) crochet hook 3·00 (no. 11).
10 buttons.
Length of shirring elastic.
The model illustrated is worked in shade 448 (Gossamer Pink).

Measurements

To fit 83·5–86·5/89–91 cm (33–34/35–36 in) bust.
Length from top of shoulder 52/53·5 cm (20½/21 in).
Sleeve seam 44·5 cm (17 in).

Tension

2 pattern repeats measure 8 cm (3¼ in).

Abbreviations   See p. 23.

Note: Work chains loosely.

Back and Fronts (worked in 1 piece to underarm)

Make 262/288 ch.

Foundation Row: 1 dc in 2nd ch from hook, 1 dc in each of next 4 ch, * 7 ch, miss 4 ch, 1 dc in each of next 9 ch; rep from * to last 9 ch, 7 ch, miss 4 ch, 1 dc in each of last 5 ch, turn with 1 ch. 19/21 patt repeats with $\frac{1}{2}$ patt at each end.

Work in patt as follows:

1st Row (right side facing):   1 dc in each of first 4 sts (turning ch does not replace first st), * 5 ch, miss 1 st, 1 dc in next ch sp, 5 ch, miss 1 st, 1 dc in each of next 7 sts; rep from * but ending last rep 1 dc in each of last 4 sts, turn with 1 ch.

2nd Row: 1 dc in each of first 3 sts, * 5 ch, miss 1 st, 1 dc in next ch sp, 1 dc in next st, 1 dc in next ch sp, 5 ch, miss 1 st, 1 dc in each of next 5 sts; rep from * but ending last rep 1 dc in each of last 3 sts, turn with 1 ch.

3rd Row: 1 dc in each of first 2 sts, * 5 ch, miss 1 st, 1 dc in next ch sp, 1 dc in each of next 3 sts, 1 dc in next ch sp, 5 ch, miss 1 st, 1 dc in each of next 3 sts; rep from * but ending last rep 1 dc in each of last 2 sts, turn with 1 ch.

4th Row: 1 dc in first st, * 5 ch, miss 1 st, 1 dc in next ch sp, 1 dc in each of next 5 sts, 1 dc in next ch sp, 5 ch, miss 1 st, 1 dc in next st; rep from * to end, turn.

5th Row: * 7 ch, 1 dc in next ch sp, 1 dc in each of next 7 sts, 1 dc in next ch sp; rep from * ending 3 ch, 1 dbl tr in last st, turn with 1 ch.

6th Row: 1 dc in first st, * 5 ch, miss 1 st, 1 dc in each of next 7 sts, 5 ch, miss 1 st, 1 dc in next ch sp; rep from * but working last dc in 4th of 7 ch, turn with 1 ch.

7th Row: 1 dc in first st, * 1 dc in next ch sp, 5 ch, miss 1 st, 1 dc in each of next 5 sts, 5 ch, miss 1 st, 1 dc in next ch sp, 1 dc in next st; rep from * to end, turn with 1 ch.

8th Row: 1 dc in each of first 2 sts, * 1 dc in next ch sp, 5 ch, miss 1 st, 1 dc in each of next 3 sts, 5 ch, miss 1 st, 1 dc in next ch sp, 1 dc in each of next 3 sts; rep from * but ending last rep 1 dc in each of last 2 sts, turn with 1 ch.

9th Row: 1 dc in each of first 3 sts, * 1 dc in next ch sp, 5 ch, miss 1 st, 1 dc in next st, 5 ch, miss 1 st, 1 dc in next ch sp, 1 dc in each of next 5 sts; rep from * but ending last rep 1 dc in each of last 3 sts, turn with 1 ch.

10th Row: 1 dc in each of first 4 sts, * 1 dc in next ch sp, 7 ch, 1 dc in next ch sp, 1 dc in each of next 7 sts; rep from * but ending last rep 1 dc in each of last 4 sts, turn with 1 ch.

These 10 rows form patt. Rep them 6 times more.

Divide for armholes and continue for right front as follows:

Next Row: 1 dc in each of first 4 sts, (5 ch, miss 1 st, 1 dc in next ch sp, 5 ch, miss 1 st, 1 dc in each of next 7 sts) 4 times, 5 ch, miss 1 st, 1 dc in next ch sp, 5 ch, miss 1 st, 1 dc in each of next 4 sts, turn with 1 ch.

4 pattern repeats with $\frac{1}{2}$ patt at each end.

Work a further 38/43 rows in patt, thus ending with 9th/4th patt row.

Continue for yoke as follows:

1st Size:

Next Row: 1 dc in each of first 2 sts, miss 1 st, 1 dc in next st, (1 dc in each of next 2 ch sps, 1 dc in each of next 7 sts, 1 dc in each of next 2 ch sps, 1 dc in each of next 3 sts, miss 1 st, 1 dc in each of next 3 sts) twice, 1 dc in each of next 2 ch sps, 1 dc in each of last 4 sts, turn with 1 ch. 43 sts. **.

2nd Size:

Next Row: 1 dc in first st, 1 dc in next ch sp, 1 dc in each of next 7 sts, (1 dc in each of next 2 ch sps, 1 dc in each of next 7 sts) 4 times, 1 dc in last ch sp, 1 dc in last st, turn with 1 ch. 47 sts.

Both Sizes:

Work 1/2 rows dc, turn with 1 ch.

Continue in dc shaping neck as follows:

1st Row: Work up to last 9/11 sts, turn with 1 ch.
2nd Row: Miss first st, work to end, turn with 1 ch.
3rd Row: Work up to last st, turn with 1 ch.

Rep 2nd and 3rd rows 4 times more. 24/26 sts.

Continue straight in dc until work measures 7 cm ($2\frac{3}{4}$ in) from beg of yoke, finishing at neck edge.

Shape shoulder as follows:

1st Row: Work up to last 5 sts, turn with 1 ch.
2nd Row: Work straight.

Rep 1st and 2nd rows 3 times more, omitting turning ch on last row.

Fasten off.

Continue for back as follows:

1st Size:

1st Row: Rejoin yarn to last st worked into on first row of right front and work another dc in this st, * 1 dc in each of next 3 sts, (5 ch, miss 1 st, 1 dc in next ch sp, 5 ch, miss 1 st, 1 dc in each of next 7 sts) 9 times, 5 ch, miss 1 st, 1 dc in next ch sp, 5 ch, miss 1 st, 1 dc in each of next 4 sts, turn with 1 ch.

9 pattern repeats with ½ pattern at each end.

Work a further 38 rows in patt, thus ending with 9th patt row. Continue for yoke as follows:

Next Row: 1 dc in each of first 4 sts, (1 dc in each of next 2 ch sps, 1 dc in each of next 3 sts, miss 1 st, 1 dc in each of next 3 sts, 1 dc in each of next 2 ch sps, 1 dc in each of next 7 sts) 4 times, 1 dc in each of next 2 ch sps, 1 dc in each of next 3 sts, miss 1 st, 1 dc in each of next 3 sts, 1 dc in each of next 2 ch sps, 1 dc in each of last 4 sts, turn with 1 ch. 86 sts.

2nd Size:

1st Row: Miss remaining 4 sts of last group worked into on first row of right front, miss 4 sts of next group, 1 dc in next st, complete as 1st row of first size from *.

Work a further 43 rows in patt, thus ending with 4th patt row. Continue for yoke as follows:

Next Row: 1 dc in first st, 2 dc in next ch sp, 1 dc in each of next 7 sts, (1 dc in each of next 2 ch sps, 1 dc in each of next 7 sts) 9 times, 2 dc in last ch sp, 1 dc in last st, turn with 1 ch. 94 sts.

Both Sizes:

Work straight in dc until back matches front at armhole edge.

Next Row: Work 25/27, place marker between last 2 sts, work 38/42, place marker between last 2 sts, work to end. Fasten off. Continue for left front as follows:

Rejoin yarn as described for corresponding size of back, work to end. Work as for right front to **.

Both Sizes:

Work 2/3 rows dc, then finish to correspond with right front.

Sleeves

Make 132/145 ch and work foundation row as for back.

9/10 patt repeats with ½ patt at each end.

Work the 10 patt rows 8 times in all, then rows 1–9 again, omitting turning ch at end of last row on 2nd size.

1st Size:

Place markers at each end of last row. Work 1 row.

2nd Size:

Next Row: Ss over 4 sts, 4 ch, miss first ch sp, 1 dc in next ch sp, patt up to last ch sp, 4 ch, ss into next st, turn.

Next Row: Ss over 2 ch, 1 dc in same ch sp, continue in patt, ending 1 dc in last ch sp.

9 patt repeats with $\frac{1}{2}$ patt at each end.

Both Sizes:

Work a further 40/43 rows in patt. Place markers at each end of last row, then work 4 more rows.

Shape as follows:

1st Row: Ss over 5 sts, (i.e. 1 dc and 4 ch) 1 dc in same ch sp, continue in pattern ending 1 dc in last ch sp, turn with 1 ch.

2nd Row: Miss first st, patt up to last st, turn with 1 ch. *3rd, 4th and 5th Rows:* As 2nd.

Rep last 5 rows once more, then 1st row again, omitting turning ch on last row. Fasten off.

Collar

Make 116/122 ch.

1st Row: 1 dc in 2nd ch from hook, 1 dc in each following ch. 115/121 sts.

Work 2 more rows in dc.

Make buttonhole in next row as follows:

Work up to last 5 sts, 2 ch, miss 2 sts, 1 dc in each of last 3 sts, turn with 1 ch.

Work 2 more rows in dc. Fasten off, turn.

Work frill as follows:

1st Row: Miss 3 sts, rejoin yarn to next st and make 1 dc, * 5 ch, miss 2 sts, 1 dc in next st; rep from * up to last 3 sts, turn.

2nd Row: 6 ch, 1 dc in next ch sp, * 5 ch, 1 dc in next ch sp; rep from * ending 3 ch, 1 tr in last st.

3rd Row: 1 dc in first st, 5 ch, miss first ch sp, 1 dc in next ch sp,

* 5 ch, 1 dc in next ch sp; rep from * up to last ch sp, 5 ch 1 dc in 3rd of 6 ch.

Rep 2nd and 3rd rows once more.

Next Row: * 6 ch, 1 dc in next ch sp; rep from * ending 3 ch, 1 tr in last st.

Next Row: 1 dc in first st, 6 ch, miss first ch sp, 1 dc in next ch sp, * 6 ch, 1 dc in next ch sp; rep from * up to last ch sp, 6 ch, 1 dc in 3rd of 6 ch.

Rep last 2 rows once more.

Next Row: * 7 ch, 1 dc in next ch sp; rep from * ending 4 ch, 1 tr in last st.

Next Row: 1 dc in first st, 7 ch, miss first ch sp, 1 dc in next ch sp, * 7 ch, 1 dc in next ch sp; rep from * up to last ch sp, 7 ch, 1 dc in 4th of 7 ch.

Rep last 2 rows once more. Fasten off.

Cuffs

With right side facing, work across free loops of starting edge of sleeve as follows:

3 dc from first $\frac{1}{2}$ group, * missing all ch sps work 7 dc from next group; rep from * to last $\frac{1}{2}$ group, 4/3 dc from last $\frac{1}{2}$ group. 70/76 sts.

Work 5 more rows in dc.

Work frill as for collar.

To make up

Join shoulder seams from markers on back.

Work 2 rows dc along lower edge. Fasten off.

Borders   (right)

With right side facing, work 120/124 dc evenly up right front edge.

Work 2 more rows in dc.

Make buttonholes as follows:

Next Row: 8 dc, * 2 ch, miss 2 sts, 10 dc; rep from * to last 4/8 sts, 2 ch, miss 2 sts, 2/6 dc.

Work 2 more rows in dc. Fasten off.

Left Front

Work 6 rows dc. Fasten off.

Sew collar to neck edge.

Insert sleeves as follows:

1st Size:

Join cuff and sleeve seams up to first set of markers, using a flat seam.

2nd Size:

Join cuff and sleeve seams using a flat seam, then sew decreased sts to missed sts of main part.

Both Sizes:

Sew sleeve top as far as markers to armhole edges at start of yoke, matching pattern. Run a gathering thread along remainder of sleeve top and gather to fit armhole; sew in position.

Thread 3 rows of shirring elastic through double crochet part of cuffs.

Sew on buttons.

Detail of Blouse

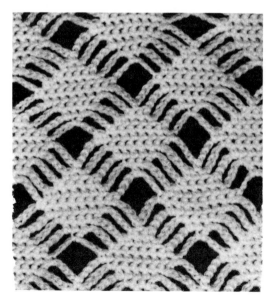

9

Baby Shawl

The simple shells radiating from the centre make a pretty shawl for the youngest member of the family.

Materials
6 (20 gram) balls of Patons Fairytale Baby 2 ply.
For perfect results, use the recommended yarn.
Milward Disc (aluminium) crochet hooks 3·50 (no. 9) and 4·00 (no. 8).
The model illustrated is worked in shade 503 (Snow-white).
Measurement
81 cm (32 in) in diameter.
Tension
6 rows – 6·5 cm (2½ in) in diameter.
Abbreviations See p. 23.

With No. 3·50 hook make 6 ch, join into a ring with ss.
1st Row: 12 dc into ring, join with ss to 1st dc.
2nd Row: 5 ch, * 1 tr in next dc, 2 ch; rep from * to end, join with ss to 3rd of 5 ch, then ss to 1st sp. 12 tr and 12 sps.
3rd Row: 3 ch, 3 tr in same sp, * 4 tr in next sp; rep from * to end, join with ss to top of 3 ch. 48 tr.
4th Row: 4 ch, 1 tr in 1st tr, miss 1 tr, * 1 tr 1 ch and 1 tr in next tr

(V made), miss 1 tr; rep from * to end, join with ss to 3rd of 4 ch, then ss to 1st ch sp.

5th Row: 1 dc in same sp, 5 ch, * miss 2 tr, 1 dc in next ch sp, 5 ch; rep from * to end, join with ss to 1st dc, then ss to 1st 5 ch sp. 24 loops.

6th Row: 3 ch, 1 tr 2 ch 2 tr in same 5 ch sp, * 2 tr 2 ch 2 tr in next 5 ch sp; rep from * to end, join with ss to top of 3 ch, then ss to 1st 2 ch sp.

7th Row: 3 ch, 1 tr 2 ch 2 tr in same 2 ch sp, * 2 tr 2 ch 2 tr in next 2 ch sp; rep from * to end, join with ss to top of 3 ch, then ss to 1st 2 ch sp.

8th Row: 1 dc in same sp, 6 ch, * 1 dc in next 2 ch sp, 6 ch; rep from * to end, join with ss to 1st dc, then ss to 1st 6 ch sp.

9th Row: 3 ch, 2 tr 2 ch 3 tr in same sp, * 3 tr 2 ch and 3 tr in next 6 ch sp (shell made); rep from * to end, join with ss to top of 3 ch.

10th Row: 3 ch, shell in sp of shell, * 1 tr in sp between 2 shells, shell in sp of shell; rep from * to end, join with ss to top of 3 ch.

11th Row: 4 ch, shell in sp of shell, 1 ch, * 1 tr in tr, 1 ch, shell in sp of shell, 1 ch; rep from * to end, join with ss to 3rd of 4 ch.

12th and 13th Rows: As 11th.

Change to No. 4·00 hook.

14th Row: 4 ch, 1 tr in same ch as 4 ch, shell in sp of shell, 1 ch, 1 tr, 1 ch, shell in sp of shell, * V in next tr, shell in sp of shell, 1 ch, 1 tr, 1 ch, shell in sp of shell; rep from * to end, join with ss to 3rd of 4 ch.

15th Row: 3 ch, V in first sp, 1 tr in next tr, shell in sp of shell, 1 ch, 1 tr, 1 ch, shell in sp of shell, * 1 tr in next tr, V in next sp, 1 tr in next tr, shell in sp of shell, 1 ch, 1 tr, 1 ch, shell in sp of shell; rep from * to end, join with ss to top of 3 ch.

16th Row: 4 ch, V in V, 1 ch, 1 tr, 1 ch, shell in sp of shell, 1 ch, 1 tr, 1 ch, shell in sp of shell, 1 ch, * 1 tr, 1 ch, V in V, 1 ch, 1 tr, 1 ch, shell in sp of shell, 1 ch, 1 tr, 1 ch, shell in sp of shell, 1 ch; rep from * to end, join with ss to 3rd of 4 ch.

17th and 18th Rows: As 16th.

19th Row: 3 ch, 1 shell in V, 1 tr, 1 ch, shell in sp of shell, 1 ch, 1 tr, 1 ch, shell in sp of shell, 1 ch, * 1 tr, 1 shell in V, 1 tr, 1 ch, shell in sp of shell, 1 ch, 1 tr, 1 ch, shell in sp of shell, 1 ch; rep from * to end, join with ss to top of 3 ch.

20th–23rd Rows: As 11th.

24th Row: 4 ch, shell in sp of shell, 1 ch, 1 tr, 1 ch, shell in sp of shell, V in next tr, shell in sp of shell, 1 ch, * 1 tr, 1 ch, shell in sp of shell, 1 ch, 1 tr, 1 ch, shell in sp of shell, V in next tr, shell in sp of shell, 1 ch; rep from * to end, join with ss to 3rd of 4 ch.

25th Row: 4 ch, shell in sp of shell, 1 ch, 1 tr, 1 ch, shell in sp of shell, 1 tr in next tr, V in next sp, 1 tr in next tr, shell in sp of shell, 1 ch, * 1 tr, 1 ch, shell in sp of shell, 1 ch, 1 tr, 1 ch, shell in sp of shell, 1 tr in next tr, V in next sp, 1 tr in next tr, shell in sp of shell, 1 ch; rep from * to end, join with ss to 3rd of 4 ch.

26th Row: 4 ch, shell in sp of shell, 1 ch, 1 tr, 1 ch, shell in sp of shell, 1 ch, 1 tr, 1 ch, V in V, 1 ch, 1 tr, 1 ch, shell in sp of shell, 1 ch, * 1 tr, 1 ch, shell in sp of shell, 1 ch, 1 tr, 1 ch, shell in sp of shell, 1 ch, 1 tr, 1 ch, V in V, 1 ch, 1 tr, 1 ch, shell in sp of shell, 1 ch; rep from * to end, join with ss to 3rd of 4 ch.

27th and 28th Rows: As 26th.

29th Row: 4 ch, shell in sp of shell, 1 ch, 1 tr, 1 ch, shell in sp of shell, 1 ch, 1 tr, 1 shell in V, 1 tr, 1 ch, shell in sp of shell, 1 ch, * (1 tr, 1 ch, shell in sp of shell, 1 ch) twice, 1 tr, 1 shell in V, 1 tr, 1 ch, shell in sp of shell, 1 ch; rep from * to end, join with ss to 3rd of 4 ch.

30th–32nd Rows: As 11th.

33rd Row: 4 ch, 1 tr in same ch as 4 ch, shell in sp of shell, * V in next tr, shell in sp of shell; rep from * to end, join with ss to 3rd of 4 ch.

34th Row: 3 ch, V in first sp, 1 tr in next tr, shell in sp of shell, * 1 tr in next tr, V in next sp, 1 tr in next tr, shell in sp of shell; rep from * to end, join with ss to top of 3 ch.

35th Row: 3 ch, V in V, 1 tr, shell in sp of shell, * 1 tr, V in V, 1 tr, shell in sp of shell; rep from * to end, join with ss to top of 3 ch.

36th and 37th Rows: As 35th, ss to 1st sp on last row.

38th Row: 4 ch, (4 dbl tr, 2 ch, 4 dbl tr) all in 2 ch sp, 1 ch, * 1 tr in V, 1 ch, (4 dbl tr, 2 ch, 4 dbl tr) all in 2 ch sp, 1 ch; rep from * to end, join with ss to 3rd of 4 ch.

39th Row: 4 ch, (4 dbl tr, 2 ch, 4 dbl tr) all in 2 ch sp, 1 ch, * 1 tr in next tr, 1 ch, (4 dbl tr, 2 ch, 4 dbl tr) all in 2 ch sp, 1 ch; rep from * to end, join with ss to 3rd of 4 ch.

40th Row: 4 ch, (5 dbl tr, 3 ch, 1 dc in 1st of these ch, 5 dbl tr) all in 2 ch sp, 1 ch, * 1 tr, 1 ch (5 dbl tr, 3 ch, 1 dc in 1st of these ch, 5 dbl tr) all in 2 ch sp, 1 ch; rep from * to end, join with ss to 3rd of 4 ch. Fasten off.

Press to size using a cool iron and dry cloth.

Detail of Baby Shawl

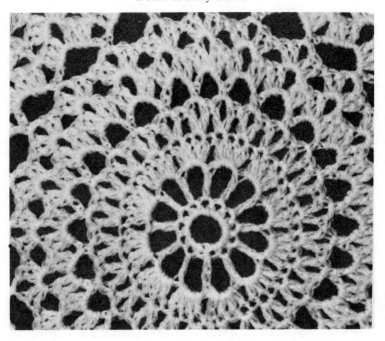

10

Baby Dresses

There is a choice with this design. The pattern can either be made as a long dress, suitable for a christening or as a short day dress.

Materials
8 (20 gram) balls of Patons Fairytale Baby 3 ply for Long Version.
6 (20 gram) balls for Short Version.
For perfect results, use the recommended yarn.
Milward Disc (aluminium) crochet hook 3·00 (no. 11).
4 buttons.
Length of ribbon.
The models illustrated are worked in shades 503 (Snow-white) and 2070 (Mermaid).
Measurements
To fit – 44·5 cm (18 in) chest.
Length from top of shoulder – 51 cm (20 in) or 35·5 cm (14 in).
Sleeve seam – 4 cm (1½ in).
Tension
5 Vs and 6 rows – 5 cm (2 in).
Abbreviations See p. 23.

Both Versions

Skirt (Worked in 1 piece from waist down)

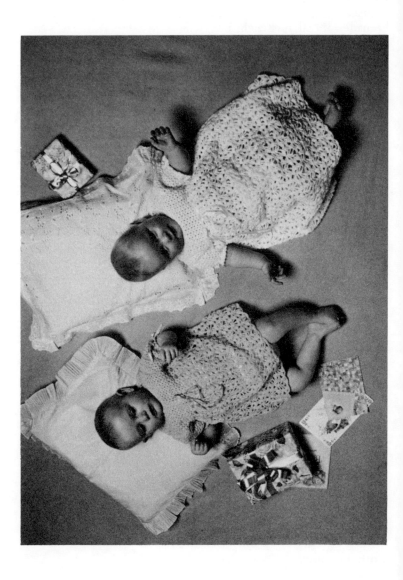

Make 193 ch.

Foundation Row: Wrong side facing, 3 tr into 5th ch from hook (a gr made), * 3 ch, miss 2 ch, 1 dc in next ch, 3 ch, miss 2 ch, 1 gr in next ch, miss 2 ch, 1 gr in next ch; rep from * to last 8 sts, 3 ch, miss 2 ch, 1 dc in next ch, 3 ch, miss 2 ch, 1 gr in next ch, miss 1 ch, 1 tr in last ch, turn with 3 ch. 21 patt repeats.

Work in skirt patt as follows:

1st Row: * Miss first 2 tr on next gr, 1 gr in next tr of gr, 4 ch, 1 dc in dc, 4 ch, 1 gr in first tr of next gr; rep from * to turning ch, 1 tr in top of turning ch, turn with 3 ch.

2nd Row: * Miss first 2 tr on next gr, 1 gr in next tr of gr, 5 ch, 1 dc in dc, 5 ch, 1 gr in first tr of next gr; rep from * to turning ch, 1 tr in top of turning ch.

3rd Row: 1 dc in first st, * 3 ch, miss 2 tr of next gr, 1 gr in next tr, 1 gr in first tr of next gr, 3 ch, 1 dc in sp between 2 grs; rep from * but working last dc in top of turning ch.

4th Row: 1 dc in first st, * 4 ch, 1 gr in first tr of next gr, 1 gr in last tr of next gr, 4 ch, 1 dc in dc; rep from * to end.

5th Row: 1 dc in first st, * 5 ch, 1 gr in first tr of next gr, 1 gr in last tr of next gr, 5 ch, 1 dc in dc; rep from * to end, turn with 5 ch.

6th Row: * 1 gr in first tr of next gr, 3 ch, 1 dc in sp between 2 grs, 3 ch, 1 gr in last tr of next gr; rep from * to turning ch, 1 trip tr in top of turning ch, turn with 3 ch.

These 6 rows form skirt patt.

Short Version:

Rep them 3 times more.

Long Version:

Rep them 6 times more.

Both Versions:

Work rows 1–3 again. Fasten off.

Bodice

With wrong side facing, rejoin yarn to base of last tr of foundation row on skirt and continue as follows:

Make 2 ch, into base of next gr work 1 tr 1 ch and 1 tr (V made), * 1 V into base of next dc, 1 V into ch sp between next 2 grs; rep from * but ending 1 V into base of last gr, miss 1 ch at side of work, 1 tr in

next ch, turn with 2 ch. 43 Vs
Continue in V patt as follows:

1st Row: * 1 V into ch sp of next V; rep from * ending 1 tr in sp between last V and turning ch, turn with 2 ch.

This row forms V patt. Keeping continuity of patt, divide for armholes and continue with right side of back as follows:

Next Row: 1 V in ch sp of each of next 8 V, 1 tr in sp before V, turn with 2 ch.

Work 11 rows more, omitting turning ch at end. Fasten off.
Continue with front as follows:

Leaving 5 V unworked, rejoin yarn to sp before next V and make 2 ch, 17 V, 1 tr in sp before next V, turn with 2 ch.

Work 7 rows more.
Shape neck as follows:

1st Row: 6 V, 1 tr, turn.

2nd Row: Ss over 4 sts, i.e. 2 tr 1 ch 1 tr, 2 ch, patt to end.

3rd Row: Patt up to last V, 1 tr, turn. 4 V remain.

Work 1 row, omitting turning ch at end.
Shape shoulder as follows:

1st Row: Ss over 4 sts, 2 ch, pattern to end.

2nd Row: Patt up to last V, 1 tr. Fasten off.

Leaving 5 V unworked, rejoin yarn to sp before next V and make 2 make 2 ch, pattern to end.

Finish to correspond with first side, reversing shapings.
Continue with left side of back as follows:

Leaving 5 V unworked, rejoin yarn to sp before next V and make 2 ch, pattern to end.

Finish to correspond with right side of back.

Sleeves

Make 57 ch.

Foundation Row: 1 V in 4th ch from hook, * miss 2 ch, 1 V in next ch; rep from * to last 2 ch, miss 1 ch, 1 tr in last ch, turn with 2 ch. 18 Vs.

Work 3 rows more in V patt. Place marker at each end at top of last row, then work a further 3 rows, omitting turning ch at end of last row.

Shape top as follows:
Ss over 4 sts, 2 ch, patt up to last V, 1 tr, turn.
Rep last row 3 times more. Fasten off.

Detail of Baby Dresses

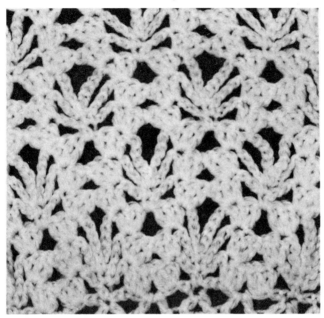

To make up

Following instructions on the ball band, press parts on wrong side.
Join shoulder seams by sewing shaped front edges to 4 Vs of straight back edge.
Join back seam of skirt matching pattern.

Borders – Neck

Starting at back opening, work in dc along left side of back and down left side of neck to start of shaping, * (3 ch, 1 dc in sp after next V) 3 times *, work in dc along straight front neck; rep from * to *, work to end.

Work picot edge as follows:

1 dc in first st, * 3 ch, 1 dc in first of these ch, miss 1 dc, 1 dc in next st; rep from * to end, (working into ch at side of neck in place of dc). Fasten off.

Back

Work 2 rows dc along each side of back opening, making 4 buttonloops in 2nd of these rows on right side, the first 2·5 cm (1 in) up from base of opening, 4th just below neck edge and remainder evenly spaced.

To make a buttonloop: 3 ch, miss 2 sts.

Sleeves

Work 1 row dc along sleeve edges, then work picot edge as for neck. Join sleeve seams up to markers, then sew remaining 3 rows to unworked sts at division for armholes. Sew remainder of sleeve top in position. Press seams and borders. Sew on buttons. Thread ribbon through first row of V pattern at yoke and sleeves.

11

All-over Crochet Pattern

The coffee table mat is a good example of this type of crochet. It shows the build up of the pattern while working in continuous rows. From the given instructions, two doilies of different sizes may also be made by working the number of rows stated in the instructions.

Coffee Table Mat and matching Doilies

Coats Chain Mercer-Crochet Cotton No. 20 (20 g).
3 balls for Coffee Table Mat.
2 balls for Doily.
1 ball for Small Doily.
These models are worked in shade 459 (Mid Sky Blue), but any other shade of Mercer-Crochet may be used.
Milward steel crochet hook 1·25 (no. 3).
Tension
First 6 rows – 5 cm (2 in) in diameter.
Measurements
Coffee Table Mat – 48 cm (19 in) in diameter.
Doily   – 38 cm (15 in) in diameter.
Small Doily   – 24 cm (9½ in) in diameter.
Abbreviations   See p. 23.

Coffee Table Mat and Matching Doilies and detail

Coffee Table Mat

Commence with 8 ch, join with ss to form a ring.

1st Row: Into ring work 16 dc, 1 ss into first dc.

2nd Row: 1 dc into same place as last ss, * 3 ch, 1 dc into next dc; rep from * ending with 1 ch, 1 hlf tr into first dc. (16 loops.)

3rd Row: * 4 ch, 1 dc into next loop; rep from * ending with 1 ch, 1 tr into hlf tr of previous row.

4th Row: * 5 ch, 1 dc into next loop; rep from * ending with 2 ch, 1 tr into tr of previous row.

5th Row: As 4th row.

6th Row: 8 ch, * 1 tr into 3rd of next 5 ch, 5 ch; rep from * ending with 1 ss into 3rd of 8 ch.

7th Row: 1 dc into same place as last ss, * 11 ch, 1 dc into same place as last dc, 5 ch, 1 dc into next tr; rep from * omitting 1 dc at end of last rep, 1 ss into first dc.

8th Row: 1 ss into each of next 5 ch, 1 dc into loop, * (5 ch, 1 dc into 5th ch from hook) 3 times (3 picots made), 1 dc into same loop, 5 ch, 1 dc into next loop; rep from * omitting 1 dc at end of last rep, 1 ss into first dc. Fasten off.

9th Row: Attach thread to centre picot of first group, 1 dc into same picot, * 9 ch, 1 dc into centre picot of next group; rep from * ending with 9 ch, 1 ss into first dc.

10th Row: 1 dc into same place as last ss, * 2 dc into next sp, 5 ch, 5 tr into same sp, 3 ch, 1 tr into next dc, 3 ch, 5 tr into next sp, 5 ch, 2 dc into same sp, 1 dc into next dc; rep from * omitting 1 dc at end of last rep, 1 ss into first dc.

11th Row: 1 dc into same place as last ss, 1 dc into next dc, * 5 ch, 2 tr into next loop, 1 tr into each of next 3 tr, (3 ch, 1 tr into next sp) twice, 3 ch, miss 2 tr, 1 tr into each of next 3 tr, 2 tr into next loop, 5 ch, miss 1 dc, 1 dc into each of next 3 dc; rep from * omitting 2 dc at end of last rep, 1 ss into first dc.

12th Row: 5 ch, * 2 tr into next loop, 1 tr into each of next 3 tr, (3 ch, 1 tr into next sp) 3 times, 3 ch, miss 2 tr, 1 tr into each of next 3 tr, 2 tr into next loop, 1 ch, miss 1 dc, 1 dbl tr into next dc, 1 ch; rep from * omitting 1 dbl tr and 1 ch at end of last rep, 1 ss into 4th of 5 ch.

13th Row: 3 ch, * 1 tr into next sp, 1 tr into each of next 3 tr, (3 ch,

1 tr into next sp) 4 times, 3 ch, miss 2 tr, 1 tr into each of next 3 tr, 1 tr into next sp, 1 tr into next dbl tr; rep from * omitting 1 tr at end of last rep, 1 ss into 3rd of 3 ch.

14th Row: 3 ch, 1 tr into each of next 2 tr, * (3 ch, 1 tr into next sp) 5 times, 3 ch, miss 2 tr, 1 tr into each of next 5 tr; rep from * omitting 3 tr at end of last rep, 1 ss into 3rd of 3 ch.

15th Row: 1 ss into next tr, 6 ch, * (1 tr into next sp, 3 ch) 6 times, miss 1 tr, 1 tr into next tr, 3 ch, miss 1 tr, 1 tr into next tr, 3 ch; rep from * omitting 1 tr and 3 ch at end of last rep, 1 ss into 3rd of 6 ch.

16th Row: 3 ch, * 4 tr into next sp, 1 tr into next tr; rep from * omitting 1 tr at end of last rep, 1 ss into 3rd of 3 ch.

17th Row: 7 ch, * miss 4 tr, 1 tr into next tr, 4 ch; rep from * ending with 1 ss into 3rd of 7 ch.

18th Row: 1 dc into same place as last ss, * 11 ch, 1 dc into same place as last dc, 4 ch, 1 dc into next tr; rep from * omitting 1 dc at end of last rep, 1 ss into first dc.

19th Row: 1 ss into each of next 5 ch, 1 dc into loop, * 5 ch, 1 dc into next loop; rep from * ending with 5 ch, 1 ss into first dc.

20th Row: 1 dc into same place as last ss, * 11 ch, 1 dc into same place as last dc, 5 ch, 1 dc into next dc; rep from * omitting 1 dc at end of last rep, 1 ss into first dc.

21st and 22nd Rows: As 19th and 20th rows.

23rd Row: 1 ss into each of next 5 ch, 1 dc into loop, * (5 ch, 1 dc into 5th ch from hook) 3 times, 1 dc into same loop, 5 ch, 1 dc into next loop; rep from * omitting 1 dc at end of last rep, 1 ss into first dc. Fasten off.

24th Row: Attach thread to centre picot of first group, 1 dc into same picot, * 7 ch, 1 dc into centre picot of next group; rep from * ending with 7 ch, 1 ss into first dc.

25th Row: 1 dc into same place as last ss, * 2 dc into next sp, 7 ch, 1 tr into next dc, 4 tr into next sp, 3 ch, 1 tr into next dc, 3 ch, 4 tr into next sp, 1 tr into next dc, 7 ch, 2 dc into next sp, 1 dc into next dc; rep from * omitting 1 dc at end of last rep, 1 ss into first dc.

26th Row: 1 dc into same place as last ss, 1 dc into next dc, * 7 ch, 2 tr into next loop, 1 tr into each of next 3 tr, (3 ch, 1 tr into next sp) twice, 3 ch, miss 2 tr, 1 tr into each of next 3 tr, 2 tr into next loop, 7 ch, miss 1 dc, 1 dc into each of next 3 dc; rep from * omitting 2 dc at end of last rep, 1 ss into first dc.

27th Row: 8 ch, * 2 tr into next loop, 1 tr into each of next 3 tr, (3 ch, 1 tr into next sp) 3 times, 3 ch, miss 2 tr, 1 tr into each of next 3 tr, 2 tr into next loop, 3 ch, miss 1 dc, 1 trip tr into next dc, 3 ch; rep from * omitting 1 trip tr and 3 ch at end of last rep, 1 ss into 5th of 8 ch.

28th Row: 3 ch, * 3 tr into next sp, 1 tr into each of next 3 tr, (3 ch, 1 tr into next sp) 4 times, 3 ch, miss 2 tr, 1 tr into each of next 3 tr, 3 tr into next sp, 1 tr into next trip tr; rep from * omitting 1 tr at end of last rep, 1 ss into 3rd of 3 ch.

29th Row: 3 ch, 1 tr into each of next 4 tr, * (3 ch, 1 tr into next sp) 5 times, 3 ch, miss 2 tr, 1 tr into each of next 9 tr; rep from * omitting 5 tr at end of last rep, 1 ss into 3rd of 3 ch.

30th Row: 3 ch, 1 tr into each of next 2 tr, * (3 ch, 1 tr into next sp) 6 times, 3 ch, miss 2 tr, 1 tr into each of next 5 tr; rep from * omitting 3 tr at end of last rep, 1 ss into 3rd of 3 ch.

31st Row: 7 ch, * (1 tr into next sp, 4 ch) 7 times, miss 2 tr, 1 tr into next tr, 4 ch; rep from * omitting 1 tr and 4 ch at end of last rep, 1 ss into 3rd of 7 ch.

32nd Row: 1 ss into each of next 2 ch, 7 ch, * 1 tr into next sp, 4 ch; rep from * ending with 1 ss into 3rd of 7 ch.

33rd and 34th Rows: As 32nd row.

35th Row: 1 ss into each of next 2 ch, 8 ch, * 1 tr into next sp, 5 ch; rep from * ending with 1 ss into 3rd of 8 ch.

36th Row: 1 ss into each of next 3 ch, 8 ch, * 1 tr into next sp, 5 ch; rep from * ending with 1 ss into 3rd of 8 ch.

37th and 38th Rows: As 36th row.

39th Row: 3 ch, * 5 tr into next sp, 1 tr into next tr; rep from * omitting 1 tr at end of last rep, 1 ss into 3rd of 3 ch.

40th Row: 8 ch, * miss 5 tr, 1 tr into next tr, 5 ch; rep from * ending with 1 ss into 3rd of 8 ch.

41st Row: 1 dc into same place as last ss, * 11 ch, 1 dc into same place as last dc, 5 ch, 1 dc into next tr; rep from * omitting 1 dc at end of last rep, 1 ss into first dc.

42nd Row: 1 ss into each of next 5 ch, 1 dc into loop, * (5 ch, 1 dc into 5th ch from hook) 3 times, 1 dc into same loop, 4 ch, 1 dc into next loop; rep from * omitting 1 dc at end of last rep, 1 ss into first dc. Fasten off.

Doily

Work same as Coffee Table Mat for 31 rows.
32nd to 34th Rows: As 16th to 18th row of Coffee Table Mat.
35th Row: As 23rd row of Coffee Table Mat having 4 ch instead of 5 ch between picot groups.

Small Doily

Work same as Coffee Table Mat for 20 rows.
21st Row: As 23rd row of Coffee Table Mat. Fasten off.

Damp and pin out to measurements.

Small Doily with insert of Doily

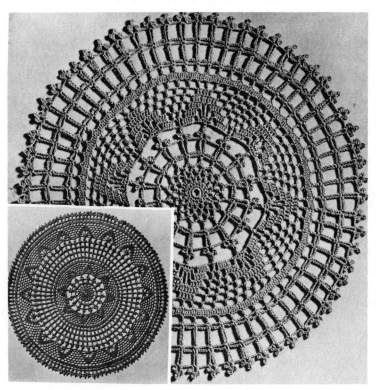

12

Crochet Motifs

Crochet motifs can be made in a variety of shapes and can be built up to make an article of any size. The tray cloth illustrated has two types of motifs which may be used independantly, if desired. Using two sections of the diagonal cross motif, with or without the small rings, a wavy pattern can be formed and this may be used to decorate the hem of a skirt or dress. The fill-in-motif may also be used as a trimming or as an all-over pattern to form many more household articles.

The motif on p. 41 can be worked in Coats Mercer-Crochet Cotton No. 20 and the size of the motif will be 4 cm (1½ in). This simple motif is most adaptable and could form the basis of tray cloths, runners, luncheon mats etc.

Tray Cloth

Coats Chain Mercer-Crochet Cotton No. 40 (20 g).
4 balls. This model is worked in shade 503 (Coral Pink), but any other shade of Mercer-Crochet may be used.
Milward steel crochet hook 1 mm (no. 4).
Size of diagonal cross – 12·5 cm (5 in) square.
Measurements
50 × 37·5 cm (20 × 15 in).
Abbreviations   See p. 23.

Diagonal Cross

First Section
Commence with 21 ch.
1st Row: 1 dc into 5th ch from hook, 1 dc into each of next 7 ch, 3 dc into next ch, 1 dc into each of next 8 ch, 4 ch, turn.
2nd Row: (Lifting back half of each st), miss first dc, 1 dc into each of next 8 dc, 3 dc into next dc, 1 dc into each of next 8 dc, 4 ch, turn.
Repeat last row 21 times more. (23 rows.) Fasten off.

Second Section
Work as first section for 22 rows. Now join as follows:
23rd Row: (Lifting back half of each st), miss first dc, * insert hook into next dc and into corresponding dc on previous section and complete as for a dc; rep from * 8 times more, complete row on second section only. Fasten off.

Third Section
Work as for previous section.

Fourth Section
Work as for previous section joining adjacent sides to form diagonal cross.

Small Ring
1st Row: Wind Mercer-Crochet 4 times round end of a pencil, remove from pencil and work 24 dc into ring, join with 1 ss into first dc.
2nd Row: 1 dc into same place as last ss, 2 ch, 1 ss into turning ch at base (to the right) of any section of cross, 2 ch, 1 dc into each of next 2 dc on ring, 2 ch, miss next 5 sts on section, 1 ss into next st, 2 ch, 1 dc into each of next 2 dc on ring, 4 ch, 1 dc into each of next 2 dc on ring, 2 ch, miss next 5 sts on section, 1 ss into next st, 2 ch, 1 dc into each of next 2 dc on ring, 2 ch, 1 ss into turning ch at base of section, 2 ch, (1 dc into each of next 2 dc on ring, 4 ch) 7 times, 1 dc into next dc, 1 ss into first dc (12 loops). Fasten off.

Make 3 more small rings joining to base of remaining 3 sections of cross. Diagonal cross completed.

Tray Cloth and detail

Make 4 more sections to form a cross. Make a small ring joining to base of any section as before and joining 10th and 11th loops to corresponding 2 loops of small ring on first diagonal cross.

Make and join another small ring to next section adjacent to first diagonal cross, joining corresponding loops as before.

Make and join 2 remaining small rings to complete cross.

Make 3 rows of 4 diagonal crosses joining adjacent small rings to corresponding loops. Where 4 small rings meet there should be one free loop between each 2 loop joinings.

Fill-In-Motifs

1st Row:　Wind Mercer-Crochet round thumb 20 times, remove from thumb and work 60 dc into ring, join with 1 ss into first dc.

2nd Row:　6 ch, leaving the last loop of each on hook work 1 trip tr into next dc, 1 dbl tr into next dc, 1 tr into next dc, 1 dc into next dc, (thread over and draw through 2 loops on hook) 4 times, * 5 ch, 1 dc into 5th ch from hook (picot made), 6 ch, 1 dc into 5th ch from hook (another picot made), 1 ch, leavng the last loop of each on hook work 1 quad tr into next dc, 1 trip tr into next dc, 1 dbl tr into next dc, 1 tr into next dc, 1 dc into next dc, (thread over and draw through 2 loops on hook) 5 times; rep from * 10 times more, 5 ch, 1 dc into 5th ch from hook, 6 ch, 1 dc into 5th ch from hook, 1 ch, 1 ss into top of first cluster.

3rd Row:　Ss to sp between picots, 12 ch, 1 dbl tr into same place as last ss, * (8 ch, 1 dbl tr into sp between next 2 picots) twice, 8 ch, into next sp between picots work 1 dbl tr 8 ch and 1 dbl tr; rep from * omitting 1 dbl tr 8 ch and 1 dbl tr at end of last rep, 1 ss into 4th of 12 ch.

4th Row:　* Into next loop work (2 dc, 4 ch) 6 times and 2 dc, 2 dc into next loop, 2 ch, 1 dc into first free turning ch loop at base of dc section of cross, 2 ch, 6 dc into same loop on fill-in-motifs, 2 ch, miss one turning ch loop of cross, 1 dc into next turning ch loop, 2 ch, 2 dc into same loop on fill-in-motif, ** (2 dc into next loop, 2 ch, 1 dc into next turning ch loop, 2 ch, 6 dc into same loop on fill-in-motif, 2 ch, miss one turning ch loop, 1 dc into next turning ch loop, 2 ch, 2 dc into same loop on fill-in-motif) twice, ** into next loop work (2 dc, 4 ch) 6 times and 2 dc, 2 dc into next loop, 2 ch, miss 3 turning ch loops, 1 dc into next turning ch loop, 2 ch, 6 dc into same loop on fill-in-motif, 2 ch, miss one turning ch loop, 1 dc into next turning ch loop, 2 ch, 2 dc into same loop on fill-in-motif *; rep from ** to ** once and from * to * once, then from ** to ** once more, 1 ss into first dc. Fasten off. Fill in all spaces in crosses in same manner.

Outer Fillings

Make necessary number of small rings and join between sections of crosses on outside edge arranging 3 small rings on each section following 'close-up' for position of joining.

Damp and pin out to measurements.

13

Crochet Edgings

Crochet lace trimmings give an expensive look to simple articles for both household or personal wear. This is also an excellent method of introducing contrast in colour, pattern or texture.

The crochet on the lunch mats has been applied to the fabric, but this design would look equally attractive if used as an edging, or an insertion.

Lunch Mats

Coats Chain Mercer-Crochet Cotton No. 20 (20 g).
2 balls. This model is worked in shade 594 (Steel Blue), but any other shade of Mercer-Crochet may be used.
Milward steel crochet hook 1·25 (no. 3).
40 cm Yellow furnishing fabric, 122 cm (48 in) wide.
The above quantity is sufficient for 2 luncheon mats.
Tension
Depth of one strip – 2·5 cm (1 in) approximately.
Measurements
Trimming – 5 × 30·5 cm (2 × 12 in) approximately.
Abbreviations   See p. 23.

Lunch Mats and detail

Place Mat

First Strip
Commence with 5 ch.

1st Row: * Leaving the last loop of each on hook work 2 tr into 5th ch from hook, thread over and draw through all loops on hook (a 2 tr cluster made), 6 ch; rep from * until work measures 48 cm (19 in) having an even number of clusters and omitting 6 ch at end of last rep. (42 clusters made.)

2nd Row: 1 dc into first cluster, * 6 ch, miss 1 ch sp, 1 dc into next 1 ch sp; rep from * along side working last dc into first ch worked, 9 ch, working along opposite side, 1 dc into next 1 ch sp, * 6 ch, miss 2 clusters, 1 dc into next 1 ch sp; rep from last * ending with 9 ch, 1 ss into first dc.

3rd Row: 4 ch, 5 dbl tr into same place as ss, remove loop from hook, insert hook into first dbl tr and draw dropped loop through (a starting popcorn st made), 2 ch, 5 dbl tr into same place as ss, remove loop from hook, insert hook into first dbl tr of dbl tr group and draw dropped loop through (a popcorn st made), 4 ch, 1 ss into same place as last ss, * 1 dc into each of next 6 ch, 1 ss into next dc, into same place as last ss work a starting popcorn st 2 ch a popcorn st 4 ch and 1 ss; rep from * along side, into next 9 ch loop work 6 dc 3 ch 1 dc into last dc – a picot made – and 5 dc, * into next 6 ch loop work 4 dc a picot and 3 dc; rep from last * along side, into next 9 ch loop work 6 dc a picot and 5 dc, 1 ss into same place as first ss. Fasten off.

Second Strip
Work as first strip for 2 rows.

3rd Row: Into same place as ss work a starting popcorn st 1 ch 1 ss into last 2 ch sp on 3rd row of first strip 1 ch a popcorn st 4 ch and 1 ss, * 1 dc into each of next 6 ch, 1 ss into next dc, into same place as ss work a starting popcorn st 1 ch 1 ss into next 2 ch sp on first strip 1 ch a popcorn st 4 ch and 1 ss; rep from * along side and complete as first strip.

Make 2 more strips joining as before.

Damp and pin out to measurements.

To make up

Cut two pieces of fabric 43 × 34·5 cm (17 × 13½ in). Turn back
1·5 cm (½ in) hems all round, mitre corners and sew hems in
position.

   Place crochet trimmings on Place Mats as shown in illustration
and sew neatly in place.

14

Pineapple Crochet

The origins of this ever popular type of crochet are uncertain. It is said to have developed from the traditional pine-cone motif found on textiles and pottery of ancient Persia and India.

This design can easily be made into many other articles by changing the number of motifs used, e.g. a runner, tray cloth, luncheon mats, etc.

Table Cloth

Coats Chain Mercer-Crochet Cotton No. 20 (20 g).
20 balls. This model is worked in shade 513 (Orange), but any other shade of Mercer-Crochet may be used.
Milward steel crochet hook 1·25 (no. 3).
Tension
Size of motif – 5·6 cm (2¼ in) in diameter.
Measurement
106·5 cm (42 in) square.
Abbreviations   See p. 23.
The above quantity is sufficient for a cloth 15 motifs × 15 motifs plus pineapple border, enlarge as desired by adding more motifs.

First Motif

Commence with 8 ch, join with ss to form a ring.

1st Row: 3 ch, 15 tr into ring, 1 ss into 3rd of 3 ch.

2nd Row: 8 ch, * 1 trip tr into next tr, 3 ch; rep from * ending with 1 ss into 5th of 8 ch.

3rd Row: 4 dc into each sp of 3 ch (64 dc), 1 ss into first dc.

4th Row: 4 ch, leaving the last loop of each on hook work 1 trip tr into each of next 4 dc, thread over and draw through all loops on hook (a cluster made), * 10 ch, leaving the last loop of each on hook work 1 trip tr into same place as last trip tr and 1 trip tr into each of next 4 dc, thread over and draw through all loops on hook (another cluster made); rep from * working last trip tr into same place as ss of previous row, 10 ch, 1 ss into top of first cluster. Fasten off.

Second Motif

Work as first motif for 3 rows.

4th Row: 4 ch, leaving the last loop of each on hook work 1 trip tr into each of next 4 dc, thread over and draw through all loops on hook, * 5 ch, 1 ss into 10 ch loop of first motif, 5 ch, 1 cluster into 2nd motif; rep from * once more and complete as first motif (no more joinings).

Make 15 rows of 15 motifs, joining each as second motif was joined to first, leaving 2 loops free between joinings.

Filling

Commence with 8 ch, join with ss to form a ring.

1st Row: 3 ch, 1 tr into ring, 5 ch, 1 ss into any free loop of motif between joinings, * 5 ch, 1 ss into top of last tr, 2 tr into ring, 5 ch, 1 ss into next free loop; rep from * 6 times more, 5 ch, 1 ss into top of last tr, 1 ss into 3rd of 3 ch. Fasten off.

Fill in all spaces in same manner.

Detail of Table Cloth

Pineapple Border

First Corner Pineapple

With right side facing, miss 3 free loops on any corner motif to left of joining, mark next loop. With wrong side facing, attach thread to centre of marked loop, 7 ch, 1 dc into next loop, 4 ch, turn.

1st Row: 10 dbl tr into 7 ch loop, 1 dbl tr where thread was attached, 5 ch, turn.

2nd Row: Miss first dbl tr, (1 dbl tr into next dbl tr, 1 ch) 10 times, 1 dbl tr into 4th of 4 ch, 6 ch, turn.

3rd Row: Miss first dbl tr, (1 dbl tr into next dbl tr, 2 ch) 10 times, miss 1 ch of turning ch, 1 dbl tr into next ch, 5 ch, turn.

4th Row: 1 dc into next 2 ch sp, (5 ch, 1 dc into next sp) 10 times, 5 ch, turn.

5th Row: 1 dc into next loop, (5 ch, 1 dc into next loop) 9 times, 5 ch, turn.

6th Row: 1 dc into next loop, (5 ch, 1 dc into next loop) 8 times, 5 ch, turn.

7th Row: 1 dc into next loop, (5 ch, 1 dc into next loop) 7 times, 5 ch, turn.

Continue in this manner, having 1 loop less on each row until row ends with 1 dc into next loop, 5 ch, 1 dc into next loop, 5 ch, turn.

Next Row: Miss 1 ch of next loop, 1 dc into next ch, 5 ch, miss 1 ch, 1 dc into next ch of same loop. Fasten off.

Second Corner Pineapple

With right side facing, miss next loop to left on same motif, mark next loop. With wrong side facing, attach thread to marked loop, 7 ch, 1 dc into next loop, 4 ch, 1 ss into last dbl tr of first row of previous pineapple, turn.

1st Row: 6 dbl tr into 7 ch loop, 1 dbl tr where thread was attached, 5 ch, turn.

2nd Row: Miss first dbl tr, (1 dbl tr into next dbl tr, 1 ch) 6 times, 1 dbl tr into top of turning ch below, 1 ss into corresponding st of previous pineapple, 4 ch, 1 ss into next loop of previous pineapple, turn.

3rd Row: 2 ch, miss next dbl tr, (1 dbl tr into next dbl tr, 2 ch) 6 times, miss 1 ch, 1 dbl tr into next ch, 5 ch, turn.

4th Row: 1 dc into next 2 ch sp, (5 ch, 1 dc into next sp) 6 times, 2 ch, 1 ss into second turning 5 ch loop on previous pineapple, 2 ch, turn.

5th Row: 1 dc into next loop, (5 ch, 1 dc into next loop) 6 times, 5 ch, turn.

6th Row: 1 dc into next loop, (5 ch, 1 dc into next loop) 5 times, 5 ch, turn.

Continue in this manner, having 1 loop less on each row and completing pineapple exactly as first corner pineapple. Fasten off.

Third Corner Pineapple

With right side facing, miss next loop to left of same motif, mark next loop. With wrong side facing, attach thread to marked loop, 7 ch, 1 dc into next loop, 4 ch, 1 ss into adjacent st of second corner pineapple, turn.

1st Row: 10 dbl tr into loop, 1 dbl tr where thread was attached, 5 ch, turn.

Complete as first corner pineapple, joining to correspond with previous joinings.

First Side Pineapple

With right side facing, miss 3 free loops to left on next motif, mark next loop. With wrong side facing, attach thread to marked loop, 7 ch, 1 dc into next loop, 4 ch, turn.

1st Row: 10 dbl tr into loop, 1 dbl tr where thread was attached, 5 ch, turn and complete as first corner pineapple, joining 2 turning ch loops of this pineapple to corresponding loops of adjacent pine-apple as before.

Make a side pineapple on each motif, joining as before. Continue in this manner all round, making 3 corner pineapples on each corner motif and taking care to join last pineapple on both sides.

Edging

1st Row: Attach thread to first free loop on first corner pineapple, 3 ch, a 2 dbl tr cluster into same loop, (7 ch, a 3 dbl tr cluster into next free loop) twice, (7 ch, into next 5 ch loop work a 3 dbl tr cluster 7 ch and a 3 dbl tr cluster) twice, (7 ch, a 3 dbl tr cluster into next loop) 3 times, a 3 dbl tr cluster into next free loop of next pineapple, 7 ch, a 3 dbl tr cluster into next loop, (7 ch, into next loop work a 3 dbl tr cluster 7 ch and a 3 dbl tr cluster) twice, (7 ch, a 3 dbl tr cluster into next loop) twice, * a 3 dbl tr cluster into next free loop on next pineapple, (7 ch, a 3 dbl tr cluster into next free loop) twice, (7 ch, into next free loop work a 3 dbl tr cluster 7 ch and a 3 dbl tr cluster) twice, (7 ch, a 3 dbl tr cluster into next free loop) 3 times; rep from * working over corner pineapple as before, join last cluster with ss to tip of first cluster.

2nd Row: Ss to centre of next loop, * 7 ch, 1 dc into next loop; rep from * round corner, ending with 1 dc into loop proceding last 2 clusters of third corner pineapple, ** 3 ch, 1 dbl tr into each of next 2 loops, 3 ch, 1 dc into next loop, (7 ch, 1 dc into next loop) 6 times; rep from ** all round, working over corner pineapples as before, ending with 3 ch, 1 dbl tr into last 7 ch loop, 1 ss into centre of first loop.

3rd Row: (9 ch, 1 dc into next loop) 22 times, * 3 ch, 1 dbl tr into each of next 2 dbl tr, 3 ch, 1 dc into next 7 ch loop, (9 ch, 1 dc into next loop) 5 times; rep from * working over corners as before and ending with 3 ch, 1 dbl tr into last dbl tr, 1 ss into centre of first loop.

4th Row: 5 ch, 1 dc into next loop, (11 ch, 1 dc into next loop) 6 times, 1 dc into next loop, (11 ch, 1 dc into next loop) 6 times, 1 dc into next loop, (11 ch, 1 dc into next loop) 6 times, * 1 ch, 1 dbl tr into each of next 2 dbl tr, 1 ch, 1 dc into next loop, (11 ch, 1 dc into next loop) 4 times; rep from * working over corners as before and ending with 1 ch, 1 dbl tr into last dbl tr, 1 ss into 4th of 5 ch.

5th Row: Ss to centre of next 11 ch loop, 1 dc into same loop, * (13 ch, 1 dc into next loop) 5 times, 1 dc into next loop; rep from * twice more, ** (13 ch, 1 dc into next loop) 3 times, 1 dc into next loop; rep from ** working over corners as before, omitting last dc at end of last repeat, 1 ss into first dc. Fasten off.

Filling between Motifs and Pineapples

Work in same manner as previous fillings working over row ends of 2nd and 3rd rows on corresponding pineapples.

Damp and pin out to measurement.

Table Cloth and detail

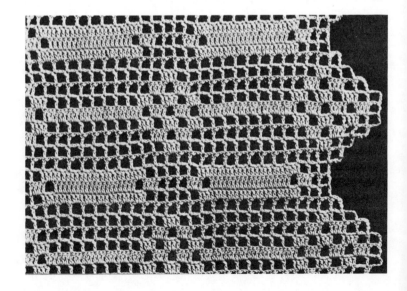

15

Filet Crochet

Filet crochet consists of a net background made from trebles and chains; the pattern being formed by solid blocks of trebles.

Filet designs are worked over a pattern of squares, therefore it is easier to follow a diagram than to read written instructions. The first few rows of the design are written, then reference is made to the diagram, which illustrates the pattern. A regular and even tension is most important as one or two loosely worked stitches can destroy the symmetry of the crochet.

By altering the number of repeats worked, the size of the table cloth can be changed or other smaller articles may be made to suit your requirements.

Table Cloth

Coats Chain Mercer-Crochet Cotton No. 20 (20 g).
10 balls. This model is worked in shade Spec. 8918 (Lt. Coral Pink), but any other shade of Mercer-Crochet may be used.
1 m fine peach fabric, 90 cm (36 in) wide.
Milward steel crochet hook 1·25 (no. 3).
Tension
5 sps and 5 rows – 2·5 cm (1 in).
Measurement
117 cm (46 in) square approximately.

Abbreviations   See p. 23.

Commence with 98 ch.

1st Row: 1 tr into 8th ch from hook, 2 ch, miss 2 ch, 1 tr into next ch (sp made), 1 tr into each of next 3 ch (blk made), (1 sp, 1 blk) twice, (2 ch, miss 2 ch, 1 tr into next ch) 8 times (8 sps made), (1 blk, 1 sp) twice, 1 blk, 8 sps, 1 blk, 1 sp, 1 blk, 5 ch, turn.

2nd Row: Miss first 3 tr, 1 tr into next tr (sp made over blk at beginning of row), 2 tr into next sp, 1 tr into next tr (blk made over sp) 2 ch, miss 2 tr, 1 tr into next tr (sp made over blk), (2 tr into next sp, 1 tr into next tr) 8 times (8 blks made over 8 sps), (1 sp, 1 blk) twice, 1 sp, 8 blks, (1 sp, 1 blk) 3 times, 2 ch, miss 2 ch, 1 tr into next ch (sp made over sp at end of row), 5 ch, turn.

3rd Row: Miss first tr, 1 tr into next tr (sp made over sp). Follow diagram to end of row.

4th Row: 1 sp, 1 blk, 10 sps, 1 blk, 1 sp, 1 blk, 10 sps, 1 blk, 1 sp, 1 blk, 2 sps, turn.

5th Row: 1 ss into each of first 4 sts (1 sp decreased), 5 ch, 1 tr into next tr, 1 sp, 1 blk and continue to follow diagram to end of row.

6th to 9th Rows: Follow diagram (Fig. 34).

10th Row: 27 sps, 5 ch, 1 tr into same place as last tr (1 sp increased at end of row), turn, 1 ss into each of first 4 sts, 7 ch.

11th Row: 1 tr into first tr (1 sp increased at beginning of row), 1 sp and continue to follow diagram to end of row.

12th Row to end: Follow diagram working to inside of heavy line at corner (2 sps remain), 5 ch, turn, turn diagram, 1 tr into same place as last tr, 2 ch, 1 tr into top of next tr, 2 tr over bar of same tr, miss 2 tr, 1 ss into each of next 4 sts, turn, 1 tr into each of next 3 tr, 2 sps, 5 ch, turn, 2 sps, 1 tr into each of next 2 tr, 1 tr into same place as ss, 2 tr over row-end, 1 tr into top of next tr, 2 tr over bar of same tr, 1 ss into top of next tr, 1 ss into each of next 3 sts, 2 ch, turn, miss 2 tr, 1 tr into next tr, 2 blks, 2 sps, 1 increase sp and continue to follow diagram to end working to inside of heavy line.

Repeat 1st to 12th row 12 times more, then 1st row to end and complete other 3 sides to correspond. Fasten off.

To make up

Oversew top of last row to foundation ch. Damp and pin out to measurements. Mount as desired.

Fig. 34

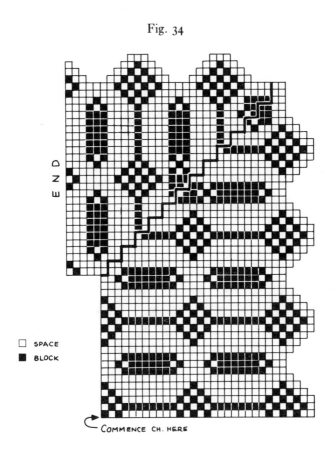

□ SPACE
■ BLOCK

COMMENCE CH. HERE

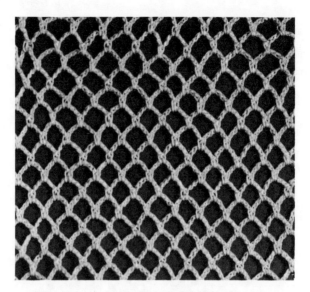

Chain Lace (above) and Loop Lace (below)

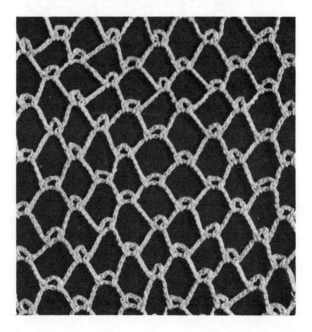

16

Irish Crochet

Irish crochet designs are different in construction from other forms of crochet and can be easily recognised by the distinctive motifs and background patterns.

This type of crochet may be worked in two ways (1) by applying the motifs to the mesh background, or (2) by working the motif first and then working the mesh background round it to form medallions, edgings or 'all-over' lace.

Instructions are given for the making of a variety of basic Irish crochet designs. The background laces are given first, then a selection of individual motifs and lastly medallions which combine motifs and background laces.

The medallions if joined together will make many articles, e.g. tea cloths, runners, chairbacks or bedspreads, and an interesting effect can be achieved by using both rose and shamrock medallions on the one article.

The pillowcase edging and insertion can easily be adapted to decorate many articles of household or personal wear.

Chain Lace

Make a chain slightly longer than desired length.

1st Row: 1 dc into 10th ch from hook, * 6 ch, miss 3 ch, 1 dc into next ch; rep from * across, 9 ch, turn.

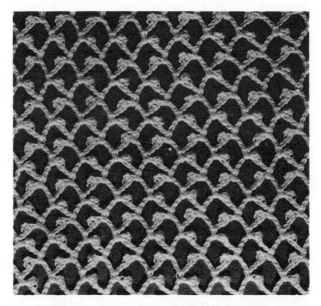

Single Picot Lace (above) and Double Picot Lace (below)

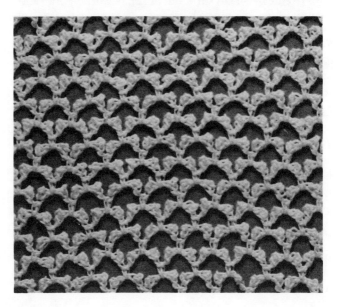

2nd Row: * 1 dc into next loop, 6 ch; rep from * across, ending with 6 ch, 1 dc into last loop, 9 ch, turn.
Rep 2nd row for length required. Fasten off.

Loop Lace

Make a chain slightly longer than desired length.
1st Row: 1 dc into 15th ch from hook, 4 ch, 1 dc into same place, * 10 ch, miss 6 ch, 1 dc 4 ch and 1 dc into next ch; rep from * across, turn.
2nd Row: Ss to centre of 4 ch loop, 13 ch, * into next 10 ch loop work 1 dc 4 ch and 1 dc, 10 ch; rep from * across, ending with 1 dc 4 ch and 1 dc into last loop, turn.
Repeat 2nd row for length required. Fasten off.

Single Picot Lace

Make a chain slightly longer than desired length.
1st Row: 1 dc into 3rd ch from hook (picot made), 2 ch, 1 dc into 8th ch from picot, * 6 ch, 1 dc into 3rd ch from hook, 2 ch, miss 4 ch, 1 dc into next ch; rep from * across, 8 ch, turn.
2nd Row: 1 dc into 3rd ch from hook, 2 ch, 1 dc into first loop (after picot), * 6 ch, 1 dc into 3rd ch from hook, 2 ch, 1 dc into next loop (after picot); rep from * across, 8 ch, turn.
Repeat 2nd row for length required. Fasten off.

Double Picot Lace

Make a chain slightly longer than desired length.
1st Row: 1 dc into 3rd ch from hook (picot made), 1 ch, 1 dc into 8th ch from picot, * 3 ch, 1 dc into 3rd ch from hook, 4 ch, 1 dc into 3rd ch from hook, 1 ch, miss 3 ch, 1 dc into next ch (picot loop made); rep from * across, 7 ch, turn.
2nd Row: 1 dc into 3rd ch from hook, 1 dc between picots of first loop, * 1 picot loop working 1 dc between picots of next loop; rep from * working last dc into loop after last picot, 7 ch, turn.
Rep 2nd row for length required. Fasten off.

Rose (1)

1st Row: Wind Mercer-Crochet 15 times round end of a pencil, remove from pencil and work 18 dc into ring, join with ss into first dc.

2nd Row: 1 dc into same place as last ss, * 4 ch, miss 2 dc, 1 dc into next dc; rep from * 4 times more, 4 ch, miss 2 dc, 1 ss into first dc. (6 loops)

3rd Row: Into each loop work 1 dc 1 hlf tr 3 tr 1 hlf tr and 1 dc, 1 ss into first dc.

4th Row: * 5 ch, 1 dc into next dc on 2nd row inserting hook from behind; rep from * 4 times more, 5 ch.

5th Row: Into each loop work 1 dc hlf tr 5 tr 1 hlf tr and 1 dc. Fasten off.

Rose (2)

Work same as 1 for 5 rows ending with 1 ss into first dc.

6th Row: * 7 ch, 1 dc into next dc on 4th row inserting hook from behind; rep from * 4 times more, 7 ch.

7th Row: Into each loop work 1 dc 1 hlf tr 6 tr 1 hlf tr and 1 dc, 1 ss into first dc.

8th Row: * 8 ch, 1 dc into next dc on 6th row inserting hook from behind; rep from * 4 times more, 8 ch.

9th Row: Into each loop work 1 dc 1 hlf tr 7 tr 1 hlf tr and 1 dc, 1 ss into first dc. Fasten off.

Single Leaf (1)

Commence with 15 ch.

1st Row: 1 dc into 2nd ch from hook, 1 dc into each ch to within last ch, 3 dc into last ch (tip of leaf), 1 dc into each ch along opposite side of foundation, 1 dc into same place as last dc. Hereafter pick up only to the back loop of each dc, 1 dc into each of next 11 dc, 1 ch, turn.

2nd Row: 1 dc into each dc to within centre dc of 3 dc group, into next dc work 1 dc 1 ch and 1 dc, 1 dc into each dc on other side to within 4 dc from centre dc at tip of leaf, 1 ch, turn.

Rose (1) and (2) (above); Single and Triple Leaf (below)

Simple Wheel and Shamrock (below)

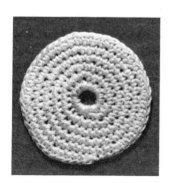

3rd and 4th Rows: 1 dc into each dc to within 1 ch, into 1 ch sp work 1 dc 1 ch and 1 dc, 1 dc into each dc on other side to within last 3 dc, 1 ch, turn.

5th Row: As 3rd row, making 7 ch instead of 1 ch.

6th Row: 1 dc into each dc to within 7 ch, into 7 ch loop work 2 dc 5 ch 3 dc 5 ch 3 dc 5 ch and 2 dc, 1 dc into each dc on other side of leaf to within last 3 dc. Fasten off.

Triple Leaf   (2)

Commence with 15 ch, hereafter work over cord (or 4 strands of same thread).

1st Row: 1 dc into 2nd ch from hook, 1 dc into each ch to within last ch, 5 dc into last ch, 1 dc into each ch along opposite side of foundation, 3 dc over cord only. Hereafter pick up only the back loop of each dc, 1 dc into each dc to within 4 dc from centre dc at tip of leaf, 1 ch, turn.

2nd Row: 1 dc into each dc to within centre of 3 dc (over cord), 3 dc into centre dc, 1 dc into each dc on other side to within 4 dc from centre dc at tip of leaf, 1 ch, turn.

3rd Row: 1 dc into each dc to within centre of 3 dc group, 3 dc into centre dc, 1 dc into each dc on other side to within last 3 dc, 1 ch, turn.

4th to 6th Rows: As 3rd row, omitting turning ch on last row. Fasten off.

Make 2 more leaves like this.

To make up
Sew sides of leaves together to form a triple leaf.

Simple Wheel

Commence with 8 ch, join with ss to form a ring. Work over a cord (or 4 strands of same thread).

1st Row: Into ring work 18 dc.

2nd to 6th Rows: 1 dc into each dc increasing 6 dc at equal distances apart (to increase – work 2 dc into 1 dc). Cut off cord, 1 ss into first dc. Fasten off.

Shamrock

Commence with 10 ch, join with ss to form a ring, (9 ch, 1 ss into same place as last ss) twice (3 rings made), into first ring work 2 dc 2 hlf tr 12 tr 2 hlf tr and 2 dc, 1 ss into same ch as last ss, (into next ring work 2 dc 2 hlf tr 12 tr 2 hlf tr and 2 dc, 1 ss into same place as last ss) twice, (picking up back loop only work 1 ss into first dc, 1 dc into each of next 18 sts, 1 ss into next dc) 3 times. Fasten off.

Rose Medallion

Commence with 8 ch, join with ss to form a ring.

1st Row: 6 ch, * 1 tr into ring, 3 ch; rep from * 4 times more, 1 ss into 3rd of 6 ch. (6 sps made.)

2nd Row: Into each sp work 1 dc 1 hlf tr 3 tr 1 hlf tr and 1 dc. (6 petals.)

3rd Row: * 5 ch, 1 dc into next tr of 1st row inserting hook from back; rep from * ending with 5 ch.

4th Row: Into each sp work 1 dc 1 hlf tr 5 tr 1 hlf tr and 1 dc.

5th Row: * 7 ch, 1 dc into next dc on 3rd row inserting hook from back; rep from * ending with 7 ch.

6th Row: Into each sp work 1 dc 1 hlf tr 7 tr 1 hlf tr and 1 dc.

7th Row: 1 dc into first dc of next petal, * 4 ch, 1 dc into 3rd ch from hook (picot made), 5 ch, 1 dc into 3rd ch from hook (another picot made), 2 ch, 1 dc into centre tr of same petal (a picot loop made), 4 ch, 1 dc into 3rd ch from hook, 5 ch, 1 dc into 3rd ch from hook, 2 ch, 1 dc into first dc of next petal; rep from * omitting 1 dc at end of last rep, 1 ss into first dc.

8th Row: Ss to centre of first picot loop (between picots), 1 dc into same loop, * 8 ch, 1 dc between picots of next picot loop, turn, 3 ch, 9 tr into 8 ch loop, 1 tr into next dc, 4 ch, turn, miss first 2 tr, 1 tr into next tr, * 1 ch, miss 1 tr, 1 tr into next tr; rep from last * twice more, 1 ch, miss 1 tr, 1 tr into top of 3 ch, 4 ch, 1 dc into 3rd ch from hook, 2 ch, 1 dc into same loop as dc after 8 ch, (4 ch, 1 dc into 3rd ch from hook, 5 ch, 1 dc into 3rd ch from hook, 2 ch, 1 dc between picots of next picot loop) twice; rep from first * omitting 1 dc at end of last rep, 1 ss into first dc.

9th Row: Ss up side of tr and into each of next 3 ch, 1 dc into sp, *4 ch, 1 dc into 3rd ch from hook, 5 ch, 1 dc into 3rd ch from hook, 2 ch, miss 1 sp, 1 dc into next sp, 4 ch, 1 dc into 3rd ch from hook, 5 ch, 1 dc into 3rd ch from hook, 2 ch, miss 2 sps, 1 dc into next loop, (4 ch, 1 dc into 3rd ch from hook, 5 ch, 1 dc into 3rd ch from hook, 2 ch, 1 dc between picots of next loop) twice, 4 ch, 1 dc into 3rd ch from hook, 5 ch, 1 dc into 3rd ch from hook, 2 ch, 1 dc into first sp of next block; rep from * omitting 1 dc at end of last repeat, 1 ss into first dc.

10th Row: Ss to centre of first picot loop, 1 dc into same loop, * 8 ch, 1 dc between picots of next loop, turn, 3 ch, 9 tr into 8 ch loop, 1 tr into next dc, 4 ch, turn, miss 2 tr, 1 tr into next tr, * 1 ch, miss 1 tr, 1 tr into next tr; rep from last * twice more, 1 ch, miss 1 tr, 1 tr into top of 3 ch, 4 ch, 1 dc into 3rd ch from hook, 2 ch, 1 dc into same loop as dc after 8 ch, (4 ch, 1 dc into 3rd ch from hook, 5 ch, 1 dc into 3rd ch from hook, 2 ch, 1 dc between picots of next loop) 4 times; rep from first * omitting 1 dc at end of last rep, 1 ss into first dc.

11th Row: Ss up side of tr and into each of next 3 ch, 1 dc into first sp, * 4 ch, 1 dc into 3rd ch from hook, 5 ch, 1 dc into 3rd ch from hook, 2 ch, miss 1 sp, 1 dc into next sp, 4 ch, 1 dc into 3rd ch from hook, 5 ch, 1 dc into 3rd ch from hook, 2 ch, miss 2 sps, 1 dc into next loop, (4 ch, 1 dc into 3rd ch from hook, 5 ch, 1 dc into 3rd ch from hook, 2 ch, 1 dc between picots of next loop) 4 times, 4 ch, 1 dc into 3rd ch from hook, 5 ch, 1 dc into 3rd ch from hook, 2 ch, 1 dc into first sp of next block; rep from * omitting 1 dc at end of last repeat, 1 ss into first dc. Fasten off.

Shamrock Medallion

Commence with 2 ch.

1st Row: 6 dc into 2nd ch from hook, 1 ss into first dc.

2nd Row: * 12 ch, miss 1 dc, 1 ss into next dc; rep from * once more, 12 ch, 1 ss into first dc.

3rd Row: Into each loop work 1 dc 1 hlf tr 15 tr 1 hlf tr and 1 dc, 1 ss into first dc.

4th Row: 1 ss into each of next 2 sts, 1 dc into next st, * (4 ch, 1 dc into 3rd ch from hook, 5 ch, 1 dc into 3rd ch from hook, 2 ch, miss 3 tr, 1 dc into next tr) 3 times, 4 ch, 1 dc into 3rd ch from hook, 5 ch, 1 dc into 3rd ch from hook, 2 ch, 1 dc into 2nd tr of next leaf; rep from * twice more, omitting 1 dc at end of last rep, 1 ss into first dc. (12 picot loops.)

5th to 8th Rows: As 8th to 11th row of Rose Medallion.

Shamrock Medallion

Pillowcase edging and detail

17

Pillowcase Edging and Insertion

Coats Chain Mercer-Crochet Cotton No. 40 (20 g).
3 balls. This model is worked in White, but any shade of Mercer-Crochet may be used.
Pillowcase.
Milward steel crochet hook 1·00 (no. 4).
Size of Motif – 5 cm (2 in) in diameter.
Measurements
Depth of Edging   – 7·5 cm (3 in).
Width of Insertion – 5 cm (2 in).
Abbreviations   See p. 23.

First Section

Commence at centre of rosette with 10 ch, join with ss to form a ring.
1st Row: Into ring work 20 dc, 1 ss into first dc.

Petal

1st Row: * 3 ch, 1 tr into next dc, 2 tr into next dc, 1 tr into each of next 2 dc, 3 ch, turn, 1 tr into first tr, 1 tr into each of next 4 tr, 2 tr into top of turning ch, 3 ch, turn, 1 tr into first tr, 1 tr into each tr and into turning ch, 3 ch, 1 dc into same place as last tr (a petal made), now work along side of petal as follows: 2 ch, 1 dc at base of 3 ch below, 2 ch, 1 ss where last tr of first row was made; rep from * working last tr on first row of 5th petal into base of first 3 ch on first petal, complete 5th petal ending with 1 tr into same place as last tr on last petal. (5 petals made.)

2nd Row: * 4 ch, 1 dc into 3rd ch from hook (picot), 5 ch, 1 dc into 3rd ch from hook, 2 ch (a picot loop made), 1 dc at tip of next petal, make another picot loop, 1 dc between centre tr of same petal, a picot loop, 1 dc at left tip of same petal; rep from * ending with 1 ss into base of first 4 ch.

Now work in rows as follows:

1st Row: Ss to sp between picots of next picot loop, * a picot loop, 1 dc between picots of next picot loop; repeat from * twice more, turn.

2nd Row: A 3 picot loop, 1 dc into next loop between picots, * a picot loop, 1 dc into next loop between picots; rep from * once more, turn.

Repeat 2nd row twice more.

5th Row: A 3 picot loop, 1 dc between picots of first loop, 7 ch, 1 dc between picots of next loop, turn, 1 ss into loop, 7 dc into same loop, 5 ch (to count as 1 tr and 2 ch) turn, 1 tr into each of next 6 dc with 2 ch between each tr (a fan made), 4 ch, 1 dc into 3rd ch from hook, 2 ch, 1 dc between picots of last picot loop, turn.

6th Row: A 3 picot loop, 1 dc into front of first tr bar of fan, * 1 dc into next 2 ch sp, 3 ch, 1 dc into same sp; rep from * 5 times more, 4 ch, 1 dc into 3rd ch from hook, 2 ch, 1 dc between next 2 picots of last loop, turn.

7th Row: A 3 picot loop, 1 dc into first 3 ch loop of fan, a picot loop, miss 3 loops of fan, 1 dc into next loop, a picot loop, 1 dc between picots of next loop, turn.

8th and 9th Rows: As 2nd row. Fasten off.

Second Section

Work as first section to within last row.

Last Row: 4 ch, 1 dc into 3rd ch from hook, 5 ch, 1 dc into 3rd ch from hook, 1 ch, miss 4 free picot loops on right side of rosette of first section, 1 dc between picots of next picot loop, * 4 ch, 1 dc into

3rd ch from hook, 2 ch, 1 dc into next loop on second section, 4 ch, 1 dc into 3rd ch from hook, 1 ch, 1 dc between picots of next picot loop on rosette of first section; rep from * once more, 4 ch, 1 dc into 3rd ch from hook, 2 ch, 1 dc into next picot loop. Fasten off. Make necessary number of sections, joining in same way.

Heading

Attach thread to 4th free picot loop of first rosette.
1st Row: 8 ch, ** 1 dc into next loop, 5 ch, 1 dc into next loop, 5 ch, 1 tr into next loop, * 5 ch, 1 dbl tr into end loop of next row; repeat from * to within next free picot loop on next rosette, 5 ch, 1 tr into next picot loop, 5 ch; rep from ** across, 1 ch, turn.
2nd Row: 7 dc into each sp. Fasten off.

Scalloped Edge

Working along opposite side, attach thread to 4th free picot loop on rosette.
1st Row: * 5 ch, 1 dc into next loop; rep from * across, turn.
2nd Row: Ss to centre of first loop, * 7 ch, 1 dc into next loop, 3 ch, turn, 14 tr into loop, 3 ch, turn, miss first tr, 1 tr into each of next 14 sts, turn, * 5 ch, miss 1 tr, 1 dc into next tr; rep from last * 6 times more, turn, * 5 ch, 1 dc into next loop; rep from last * 6 times more, 1 dc into next loop (on first row of scalloped edge), 7 ch, 1 dc into next loop; rep from first * across, turn.
3rd Row: Ss to centre of first loop, 1 dc into same loop, 2 ch, 1 dc into next loop, * 5 ch, 1 dc into next loop; rep from * 5 times more, 5 ch, 1 dc into first loop on next scallop; rep from first * across. Fasten off.

To make up

Sew narrow ends together, matching pattern.

Insertion

Work as edging, making heading on both long sides. Sew narrow ends together. Pin insertion in place 8·8 cm ($3\frac{1}{2}$ in) from edge of pillowcase. Cut away material at back of insertion, leaving 3 mm ($\frac{1}{8}$ in) for hem on each side. Sew hems and insertion neatly in place. Sew on edging.

Damp and press.

18

Hairpin Lace

Hairpin lace is a most charming type of crochet, having a delicate and fragile appearance. The example which we have given on p. 115 is for an edging for a handkerchief, but, by using a heavier yarn, a larger staple and the appropriate hook, a wider edging can be made, suitable for trimming a number of articles of household and personal wear.

How to Work the Lace

Use a crochet hook and hairpin lace staple. Hold the crochet hook in the right hand. Make a loop at end of ball thread and slip on to crochet hook. Take the hairpin in the left hand and hold it flat between the thumb and first finger, with prong end uppermost and the round part downwards in the palm of the hand (see Steps 1 to 7).

Step 1   Make a loop at end of ball thread (Fig. 35).

Step 2   Insert hook in loop and wind ball thread around right prong of hairpin (Fig. 35).

Step 3   Thread over hook and draw through loop, keeping loop at centre (Fig. 35).

Step 4   Raise hook to a vertical position and turn hairpin to the left (Fig. 36).

Step 5   Thread over hook and draw through loop on hook (Fig. 37).

Step 6   Insert hook into loop of left prong (Fig. 38).

Step 7   Thread over hook and draw loop through (2 loops on hook), thread over and draw through remaining 2 loops.

Repeat steps 4 to 7 for length required.

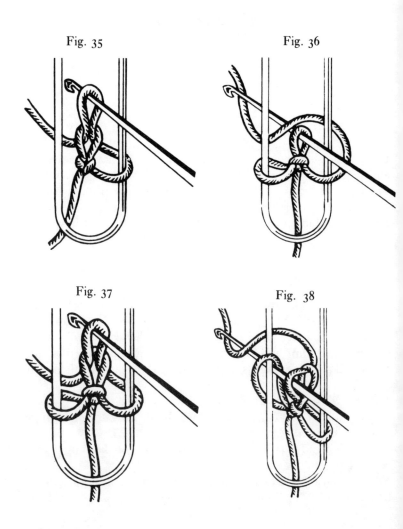

Fig. 35

Fig. 36

Fig. 37

Fig. 38

19

Edging for a Handkerchief

Coats Chain Mercer-Crochet Cotton No. 40 (20 g).
1 ball. This model is worked in White, but any shade of Mercer-Crochet may be used.
Milward steel crochet hook 1·00 (no. 4).
Hairpin lace staple 1·3 cm ($\frac{1}{2}$ in) wide.
Handkerchief.
Measurement
Depth of edging – 2·5 cm (1 in).
Abbreviations   See p. 23.

How to Work the Lace

See p. 113–4 for steps 1 to 7.
Work a piece of hairpin lace for length required plus 2·5 cm (1 in) for each corner, having a multiple of 5 loops for each side and 10 loops for each corner.
Join at centre and fasten off.
Keep loops twisted throughout.

Edging

Attach thread to first 5 loops, 1 dc into same place, * 5 ch, into last dc work 1 ss 7 ch 1 ss 5 ch and 1 ss (a triple picot made), 7 ch, 1 ss

Handkerchief edging and detail

into 5th ch from hook, 3 ch (a picot loop made), 1 dc into next 5 loops; rep from * to corner omitting picot loop and 1 dc at end of last rep, 8 ch, 1 ss into 5th ch from hook, 4 ch (a corner picot loop made), 1 dc into next 5 loops; rep from first * omitting 1 dc at end of last rep, 1 ss into first dc. Fasten off.

Heading

With right side facing, attach thread to 6th loop on opposite side after any corner, 1 dc into same place as join, * 1 dc into each loop to within group before next corner picot loop, (1 dc into next 5 loops) twice (a corner made); rep from * ending with 1 ss into first dc. Fasten off.

Damp and press

Sew neatly to edge of handkerchief.

Index

EMBROIDERY

LYNETTE DE DENNE

Embroidery is a very ancient and beautiful art using many different techniques which reflect the life of the periods in which they were developed. Today, the embroiderer can make use of all these different styles and produce work of great variety and originality, often by mixing techniques: patchwork can appear as part of a wall hanging, canvas work be applied to another background with other stitchery.

This book gives clear step-by-step instructions on the different techniques and how they can be used and is fully illustrated throughout. Lynette de Denne has also included useful advice on buying material and threads and ideas for making your own embroidery designs.

This is the basis the beginner needs when starting to embroider and with it you will be able to find out what you enjoy most and to start adapting or combining the different techniques to your individual designs. A well-planned, simple, original embroidery can often be as effective as intricate and sophisticated work.

Lynette de Denne is an Embroidery Consultant and an editor of *Embroidery*.

TEACH YOURSELF BOOKS

KNITTING

WINIFRED BUTLER

This book is a comprehensive guide, with clear diagrams and sound advice so that learners can become experts.

It covers the choice of materials, step-by-step instructions on basic stitches, increasing and decreasing, how to cast off and on, and how to join wool. Patterns include those which can be knitted by the beginner with variations to cover knitwear, baby wear, bedspreads and cushions.

Winifred Butler is an acknowledged expert in the art of knitting and has been Knitting Editor of a leading woman's magazine for many years.

TEACH YOURSELF BOOKS

DRESSMAKING

ISABEL HORNER

Dressmaking can be a very enjoyable way of keeping yourself in fashionable but inexpensive clothes. It can also be a way of appearing in a dress that only too obviously has been 'run up in a few hours'.

With this book even the beginner can avoid the usual pitfalls of home dressmaking and will be able to make very attractive, yet economical clothes.

Initial chapters on equipment, patterns and materials are followed by step-by-step instructions on each stage of dressmaking: cutting out, tacking up, fitting, fastenings, trimmings etc. The author also includes advice on renovation and remodelling and the care and repair of clothes.

Although intended primarily for the beginner, this book will be useful as a source of reference and ideas to the more experienced dressmaker.

TEACH YOURSELF BOOKS

HANDWRITING

JOHN Le F. DUMPLETON

**The necessary skills for beautiful handwriting
can be acquired after only a few hours of
practice.**

This book enables you to create an attractive, legible
and speedy handwriting without losing your
individual style. It is achieved through a series of
exercises which can transform even the most illegible
of scrawls following the over one hundred examples
laid out in the text.

TEACH YOURSELF BOOKS

CREATIVE WRITING

VICTOR JONES

How can one learn to write creatively, for, as the author of this book writes, 'to suggest that a book on creative writing can create a creative writer is equivalent to suggesting that a book on divinity can create God'.

But what the aspiring writer can do is to recognise that he, like everyone else, enjoys the essential attributes of the writer—experience of life and native talent.

This book demonstrates how to shape and control this talent, drawing on one's own personal experience. It covers every form of writing, from the novel and the short story to poetry, drama and writing for radio and television.

The result is an approach to creative writing, packed with practical advice on how to find both success and satisfaction in one's own work.

TEACH YOURSELF BOOKS